Best of British
FISH &
SEAFOOD

Lesley Ellis

**DIAL
HOUSE**

CONTENTS

First published 1995

ISBN 0 7110 2300 X

Published by Dial House

an imprint of Ian Allan Ltd, Terminal House, Station Approach, Shepperton, Surrey TW17 8AS.
Printed by Ian Allan Printing Ltd, Coombelands House, Coombelands Lane, Addlestone, Weybridge, Surrey KT15 1HY.

Previous page: Whole and Bon Kippers.
Food Features

Introduction

We are an island nation, so it is not surprising we have always caught and eaten fish, and that some of the best British traditional and regional foods are based on fish and seafood — Scottish smoked salmon, wild Welsh sea trout, Cromer crab, Whitstable oysters, potted shrimps from Morecambe Bay, quaintly named Cornish star-gazey pie, jellied eels, Manx kippers, Finnan haddie...and of course fish and chips.

British fisheries have always been abundant and in spite of upheavals in recent years, the industry is still a major provider of food: in 1993 the fishing fleet landed more than 600,000 tonnes of fish and seafood — mackerel, herring, cod, plaice...as well as shellfish and more unusual species such as monkfish, gurnard and brill.

It is a strange fact that in the face of all this bounty, we are as a nation very conservative about buying and cooking fish. We enjoy haddock and cod and the occasional kipper, but how often do most of us bring home pollack or sea bream for supper?

Time and again, people in the industry tell the same story, that much of our best Sea Fish disappears off to markets abroad because there is insufficient demand at home. And the same is true of freshwater fish. The British have a prejudice against it

Seafish Industry Authority

3

and so it is not available in most shops, yet carp and pike and eel are all considered great eating in other countries.

Things are starting to change. People in Britain are becoming more discerning about the food they eat, its quality, freshness and nutritional content. Many of the major supermarkets now run excellent fish counters with a good range of fish and knowledgeable staff. Indeed, I find most fishmongers to be a fund of enthusiastic information on cooking and preparing different species, so I never mind asking advice.

Some people worry about the bones in fish, but fishmongers will always fillet these out if given a bit of notice in busy periods, and if you cannot cope with leery-eyed fishheads ask for these to be removed too. People also complain that fish is expensive and it is true that some kinds are — turbot, Dover sole, lobster...these are special fish for special occasions, but there are also lots of cheaper varieties, not only coley but ling, pollack, mackerel, herrings, sprats and whitebait, all economical, all interesting to try.

For anyone whose only contact with fish is by way of a frozen cod steak, a simply grilled fresh fillet, with a little black pepper and dotted with butter, will come as a culinary revelation. We have seen a renaissance in real British cheeses and real British ales in recent years; it now seems time for a real fish revival.

Food Features

FISH AND SEAFOODS — A BRIEF GUIDE

Sea Fish can be divided into three groups: White fish, Oil-rich fish, and Shellfish. Freshwater fish have their own section in this book.

White fish

These are different from the oil-rich fish because their oil is not in the flesh but concentrated in the liver. The flesh of white fish is low in fat and calories.

White fish can be divided into round fish and flat-fish. (These are not scientific classifications as used here — skate, for example, can be scientifically classified with sharks and dogfish (huss) because, like them, it has a cartilaginous skeleton, but here it is included in the flat-fish group, because that is the way it is cooked.)

The majority of white fish we eat comes from that important family of round fish, the cod group — cod, haddock, saithe (coley), whiting, hake, pollack and ling. These are usually sold as fillets, cutlets or steaks, though smaller fish, such as whiting, are sold whole.

The most popular flat-fish in Britain is plaice. Small flat-fish like plaice are usually sold whole or in fillets; larger species such as halibut are sold as cutlets or quarter-cut fillets.

Oil-rich fish

There has been a lot of publicity in the last few years about the health benefits of eating oil-rich fish. The oil is dispersed throughout the flesh in

Left: Trawler at work in the North Sea. The fishing industry has its origins back in prehistoric times when coastal fishermen first fished with hooks and lines from small boats, as well as using spears, basket traps and tidal fish barriers. Fishing techniques were still quite primitive when the Romans arrived; they introduced drift net fishing for herring, and also brought the first fishfarming to Britain, artificially raising native oysters (for which they had a passion).

The Icelandic cod fisheries developed in the 15th century, and remained important to Britain for 500 years, until the cod war with Iceland in the 1970s put an end to our long-distance deep-sea fishing industry. Today, British boats work mainly European Community waters, and smaller family vessels have taken over from the great company fleets — the North Sea and the west coast of Scotland are our most important waters.

Sadly, pollution and overfishing have taken their toll on fish stocks throughout the world, and Britain, like other countries, now has to abide by strict fishing quotas to help conserve supplies. Once-cheap fish, such as hake and cod, are scarcer and more expensive, although not all species have suffered; for some, such as trout, salmon and mussels, prices have tumbled thanks to recent developments in fishfarming. Who would have dreamt 10 years ago, that you could buy a salmon for the price of cod?
Seafish Industry Authority

Above:
An array of seafish, smoked fish and shellfish — turbot, brill, halibut, pollack,
haddock, hake, coley, lemon sole, whiting, herring, mackerel, squid, witch,
kippers, finnan haddock, kipper fillets, undyed golden cutlets, smoked

haddock, peppered mackerel and mackerel fillets, monkfish tails, cod cutlets and fillets, plaice fillets, skate, Pacific oysters, king scallops, mussels, cockles, shelled prawns, Dublin Bay prawns, lobsters, unshelled prawns and shelled mussels. *Seafish Industry Authority*

these fish, is rich in vitamins A and D, and is polyunsaturated, so is a healthy alternative to the saturated fats in most meats.

Fish oil is also a source of polyunsaturates known as omega-3 fatty acids, and medical research has shown that if these are

Above:
Feeding salmon in a Scottish sea-loch fish farm.
Scottish Salmon Board

included in a diet, they can help prevent serious illnesses such as heart disease, strokes and arthritis. They are also important during pregnancy. Research suggests that we should be eating 3-7 grams of omega-3s each week in our diet.

HOW MUCH OMEGA-3S DO DIFFERENT SEAFOODS CONTAIN?

(PER 4OZ/100GM EDIBLE PORTION)
- mackerel   2.0–4.0gm
- sprats   2.0–3.0gm
- sardines   2.0–2.5gm
- herring   1.5–2.0gm
- salmon (canned)   1.5–2.0gm
- salmon (smoked)   1.0–1.5gm
- halibut   0.7–1.0gm
- trout   0.5–1.0gm
- lobster   0.3–0.5gm
- cod (steamed)   0.2–0.3gm
- haddock (fried)   0.2–0.3gm
- prawns   0.2–0.3gm

(data supplied by the Fish Foundation)

Oil-rich fish, such as mackerel, herring and sprats, are usually sold whole.

Freshwater fish

Trout and salmon are the most popular freshwater fish in Britain today — fish-farming technology has dramatically cut the price of these once luxury foods, and whole salmon is now often to be found at less than the price of cod. Athough always described as freshwater species, wild salmon, sea trout and eels all spend part of their lives in the sea.

Shellfish

These are divided into crustaceans (shellfish with legs such as lobsters and shrimps) and molluscs (those without legs, such as winkles and oysters). Then there are the cephalopods — squid and octopus, which although they have lost all or most of their shell during evolution, really do belong with the shellfish, both scientifically and from a culinary point of view.

Smoked fish

Fish is a perishable food, so it has always been important to have ways of preserving it, by smoking, salting,

Clams, razor-shells, winkles, Pacific oysters, king scallops, whelks, queen scallops, mussels and princess scallops: all molluscs. *Seafish Industry Authority*

drying or pickling. Now that we have refrigeration and canning, traditional techniques have become redundant, but are still used because of the interesting flavours they impart. Smoking is especially popular: the two main methods are hot-smoking, which cooks the fish through; and cold-smoking, which gives a delicate smoky flavour but leaves the fish essentially raw.

Seaweeds

Not many people in Britain eat seaweed these days, but at one time it played a part in many people's diets. There are several species that have been used over the years; some still are harvested and eaten locally, so anyone turning food detective can probably hunt some out.

Below: Flat-fish can be divided into right-facing species and left-facing species — a useful aid to identifying the different varieties. Plaice and lemon sole look to the right; turbot looks to the left.
Seafish Industry Authority

BUYING FISH AND SEAFOOD

Most fish and seafood that we eat are caught from the wild, which means they are a completely natural food with no artificial additives. But it also means that supplies are dependent on the whims of nature and that scarcities or gluts can bring dramatic changes in price. High prices are not necessarily a good indication of top quality when you are buying fish; in fact, most kinds of fish are at their best when they are in season and cheap. To get the best from your fishmonger's shop, be prepared to experiment, buying whatever is at its best.

Most fish should be cooked as soon as possible after landing, though certain species improve with keeping for a day or two — wild salmon, grey mullet, John Dory, Dover sole, shark, skate. This is partly a matter of taste, but consult your fishmonger and remember: fish may already be a couple of days old when it arrives at the monger's; that freshness is also dependent on how the fish has been kept on board and during transport from the docks; and that no fish should be eaten if it is stale, or smells 'off'. Your best guarantee is always to go to a reputable supplier, where the produce is kept, displayed and handled properly.

To check for absolute freshness and quality, look for the following:

Whole fish
- plump firm specimens.
- bright clear, unsunken eyes.
- glistening, moist skin with clear colours.
- bright pink gills.
- firmly attached scales.
- clean pleasant smell.
- choose thicker specimens of flatfish where possible.

Fillets, Steaks and Cutlets
- firm, springy flesh, never spongy.
- translucent colour, not milky or discoloured.
- moist flesh, but no slime or signs of drying around the edges.
- choose thicker fillets for moistness and meatiness (dark-skinned, upper fillets of flat- fish are thicker than light-skinned under fillets).
- clean pleasant smell, without unpleasant 'fishy' odour. (Skate, rays, shark and dogfish (huss) all smell ammoniacal when freshly caught. This is normal and disappears within a day or two of landing; any residual smell goes with cooking.)

Frozen Fish
- shops with a brisk turnover.
- properly sealed bags, odourless, unpunctured and fresh looking.
- properly frozen packages, not soft or slushy.
- no accumulation of ice around packages or fish.

Above: Baking fish *en papillote*, in paper or foil, keeps in all the natural moisture. Seal the package tightly by twisting up the ends. Here, the method has been used to cook fillet of lemon sole. *Seafish Industry Authority*

- no whitish 'freezer burn' marks on fish.
- all packages within their sell-by date.

Cans and Bottles

- undamaged, undented containers in good condition, still properly sealed.
- all products within their sell-by date.

Shellfish; Cooked

- undamaged, uncracked shells, never soft.

- lobsters and crabs which feel heavy for their size.
- properly chilled, freshly cooked prawns and shrimps which feel firm to touch.

Shellfish; Live

- no detectable smell.
- specimens kept in cool, moist conditions.
- bivalves, such as mussels and oysters, all tightly shut or will shut quickly when tapped.
- bivalve shells not too heavy for

their size, or they will probably be dead, and full of sand.

Smoked Fish

- pleasant smoky aroma.
- bright, shiny appearance, never matt or dried out.
- firm flesh, not soggy.

CATCHING AND GATHERING YOUR OWN

If you want to catch your own fish, or gather shellfish and other seafoods, it is important to:

- Make sure you have the necessary licence to fish in any water and that you are not fishing out of season — details from local river authority.

- Always check that the shore or river where you fish or gather is a safe place to be, without dangerous tides or mudflats.

- Make sure that the river or shoreline is unpolluted: check with the appropriate river or harbour authority, or the local authority environmental health officer. Never harvest shellfish from shores near conurbations or factory outflows.

- Do not gather shellfish during summer months, when they are breeding and out of condition. Avoid gathering mussels altogether, or if you must collect them, remember that the east coast is liable to natural but toxic 'red tides' in spring and summer.

- Never take spats (undeveloped shellfish), only full-grown specimens. Throw back undersized fish.

- Always take a reliable field guide when gathering seaweeds. Make absolutely sure you correctly identify edible seaweeds — some species are *inedible*.

- Never strip an area; leave as much as you take.

- Make sure you do not disturb rare or protected species.

- Discard old or damaged specimens of shellfish or seaweeds.

- Discard open shellfish, which will not close when sharply tapped.

- Discard all doubtful-smelling specimens.

- Clean fish as soon as possible after catching.

- Wash all shellfish and seaweeds thoroughly in clean water. Allow to soak for at least five hours, changing water several times, before cooking.

- After cooking, discard all shellfish that remain shut.

DISPATCHING LIVE SHELLFISH HUMANELY

Crabs and lobsters are sometimes sold live. Eels can also be bought live from specialist fish shops, but I strongly recommend you do not try killing these yourself; research shows it is hard to do humanely; leave it to the experts.

You may decide that it is better not to buy live crabs and lobsters either if they have been under the stress of long hours of display on the fish counter, but if you do buy them follow the RSPCA's recommended methods for humane killing. Place the shellfish in the freezer before cooking — for at least two hours at -4°F (-20°C): they will then be comatose when it comes to cooking. Alternatively, plunge them in a large volume of rapidly boiling water, to ensure instant death.

PREPARING FISH

Scaling fish

This is easy, but a bit messy. Your fishmonger will do it, if you don't want to.
• Hold fish by its tail. Take a stout knife and stroke the *blunt* edge of it firmly down the fish from tail to head, against the lie of the scales.
• Wash fish under running water.
• Some fish, such as perch, have firmly attached scales. If you have difficulty scaling a fish, plunge it in boiling water for a few moments, and the scales should come away easily.

Tails, heads and fins

• Cut off the tail with a sharp knife; clip off fins and spines with strong scissors.
• To remove head before cooking, cut through the fish just below the gills. If leaving the head on, remove gills as these produce a bitter taste.

Cleaning a fish

This is another job the fishmonger will undertake, though quite easy to do. A fish can be cleaned with or without the head on. If removing head, do this first.
• Lay fish on its side. With a sharp knife, make an incision, below the gills if head is still on, and slice two-thirds of the way along the belly.
• Scrape out innards and wash cavity.

Filleting and skinning round fish

Again, a job your fishmonger will do if given notice, but not difficult with a sharp knife.
• Holding the cleaned fish firmly, slice along the back, from head to tail, cutting deeply enough to expose the backbone.
• Now detach the fillet from head end by cutting just below gills.
• Insert knife at this point and slice horizontally to cut the fillet away from the bones, working from head to tail.
• Turn fish over and repeat process.
• To remove the skin, lay fillets skin-side down. Cut off about ½in (1cm) of flesh from tail end, leaving a small flap of skin.
• Secure the fillet by pressing down on this flap, then insert a sharp knife between flesh and skin and cut between the two, using short sawing strokes.

Skinning flat-fish

The dark skin of flat-fish is usually removed; the light skin just scaled.

- Place fish dark skin uppermost. Cut off tail. Using a knife, release a little flap of skin at this point.
- Hold this flap in one hand, press down on exposed flesh with the other, then tug skin up and away from the flesh.

To fillet a small flat-fish

This can be done before skinning.

- Remove head, fins and tail.
- Insert knife at head end. With horizontal sawing motion, slice fillet from bone.
- Do not turn fish over, but repeat process, cutting under the backbone to release second fillet.
- Large flat-fish are usually filleted into four quarter-fillets, two each side of the fish.

Boning a round fish

This method is useful if stuffing a whole fish:

- Remove fins and gills. Clean the fish.
- Lengthen opening in the belly of the fish and open it out flat, skin-side down.
- Prise out and snip off the ribs, using scissors.
- Run a sharp knife down each side of the backbone, then cut it free from tail and head with scissors. This method is good for herring and trout:
- Remove, head, fins and tail and clean fish.
- Lengthen the opening in the belly

Above: Poaching is a gentle method, ideal for white fish, delicate seafood and salmon. Here, scallops are poached briefly in milk, the poaching liquor then seasoned and thickened, and the mixture browned in the oven.
Seafish Industry Authority

THE GREAT BRITISH TAKE-AWAY

Fish and chips first appeared in the 19th century — the perfect take-away food for working families of the newly industrialised towns. In the early days of fried fish shops, the fish was sold with a fat slice of bread or jacket potato, then the French invented chips and by the 1850s or 1860s (depending on which source you believe) the first proper fish and chip shops were in business.

Where in Britain can you get the best fish and chips? The best I have tasted were from Whitby, North Yorkshire — fresh local haddock, fried to order, munched crisp and succulent straight from the paper. Indisputably the most famous chip shop in the world is in Yorkshire — Harry Ramsden's at Guiseley, north of Leeds. Established in 1928 in a hut no bigger than a garden shed (*Right*: Harry Ramsden's), today the Guiseley establishment seats 250 beneath cut-glass chandeliers, with branches as far afield as Hong Kong. In true northern style, Harry Ramsden's serves haddock and chips, plaice and chips and halibut and chips, but no cod.

If you are cooking at home, the key to fish and chip perfection is to twice-fry the chips, in smoking-hot oil (360°F/190°C). The first frying cooks the chips through, then the second frying (after you have fried the fish at 350°F/180°C) browns and crisps them. The batter must coat the fish thinly, but completely, so the fish steams in its own juices. Fish and chips are excellent with crisp green salad and a glass of white wine, but also good the traditional way, with brown bread and butter and cups of tea. *Seafish Industry Authority*

Above: Fish and chips. Seafish Industry Authority

of the fish and open it out on the work surface, skin-side up.

- Using both thumbs, press down firmly either side of the backbone to release it from the flesh. Work down the length of the fish.
- Turn fish over and carefully pull out the backbone and ribs.

COOKING FISH

Whatever method you use, always cook fish gently and never overcook it. It is done when the flesh turns from translucent to opaque and comes away from the bone.

POACHING

Barely cover the fish with warm stock, wine, cider or milk, then cook on a low heat (or in preheated oven). Do not allow above a bare simmer. Fish to be eaten cold can be placed in cold stock, brought to a simmer, then the heat turned out. The fish finishes cooking as it cools in the liquid.

BAKING AND ROASTING

This retains all the natural juices and vitamins. The seasoned fish is moistened with butter or oil and a little liquid and basted frequently during cooking.

BRAISING

The fish is cooked on a bed of sautéed vegetables in the oven, giving extra flavour and moisture. Liquid is added to cover the vegetables and it is all sealed with a tight lid or foil.

GRILLING AND BARBECUING

A good method for small whole fish, fillets and steaks. Make diagonal slashes in round fish to enable heat to penetrate evenly. Use a medium heat and baste regularly to keep moist.

Barbecuing is ideal for oily fish such as herring and mackerel. Marinate firm-fleshed fish such as monkfish for skewering on kebabs.

STEAMING

This is a delicate method of cooking, good for fillets. If you don't have a steaming basket, place the seasoned, buttered fish between two plates over a saucepan of simmering water.

FRYING

Use good quality clean oil (or butter for shallow-frying). If deep-frying, always seal fish in coating of egg and breadcrumb, batter or seasoned flour. Make sure oil is properly pre-heated and batch-fry to prevent overcrowding the pan. Drain cooked fish well on paper towel before serving.

MICROWAVING

This is an easy way to cook fish perfectly every time. Cooking time varies according to thickness and quantity of fish. You will need only a little added liquid using this method.

ROUND WHITE FISH

THE COD FAMILY

Cod, haddock, whiting, hake, coley, ling and pollack are all members of the cod family, white fish mainly of cold northern waters. Britain's fishing fleet catches more of these than any other species except mackerel, and they are far and away the industry's most valuable haul. As a nation, we may not be eating nearly as much fish as we used to, but we have kept our taste for cod, haddock and coley — though we now eat a lot

of it in pre-prepared forms: frozen, crumbed, coated, battered, buttered, and encased in pies.

COD

Cod, the most important member of the cod family, is the favourite fish in Britain — we have been eating it since late prehistoric times, and by the early 15th century fishermen were venturing out in little ketches as far as Iceland in search of it.

These are fish of the cold northern oceans — the North Atlantic and Arctic — where they usually live down in the chilly depths. Some people say that the colder the water is, the better the quality of the fish. Quite big cod are caught all around the coast by sports anglers.

Britain's main commercial cod fisheries are in the North Sea and west of Scotland, although we also catch some from the Norwegian coast, the English Channel and off the Irish coast and the Faroes.

The cod is a handsome fish, growing to 40in (1m) or more in length with a distinctive barbel on its chin and a speckled skin. Iceland cod is usually dark brown, Faroe cod paler and the cod caught off northwest Scotland and Norway a deep red or bronze. You won't see a large whole fish in the fishmonger — you're more likely to find fillets, cutlets or (smaller)

Left: Haddock, whole fish and fillet.
Food Features

Left: Cod, whole fish and fillet.
Food Features

ROES
— AND WHAT TO DO WITH THEM

Fresh cod's roes are available through winter and into spring; fishmongers sometimes sell them ready-cooked, but if you want to try cooking some yourself, wrap them in a pudding cloth, or greaseproof paper to prevent them bursting, then poach gently. Leave to cool, then cut into ½in (1cm) slices and fry in butter, dusted with seasoned flour. It makes a good breakfast. Alternatively, make fishcakes: Dorothy Hartley's version of a 14th-century English recipe mixes the cooked roe with a little sugar, salt, pepper, cream cheese (use just enough to bind without getting sticky). Form the cakes, then coat in batter or breadcrumbs and fry gently. Canned cod's roe, ready-cooked, is convenient and slices beautifully. Haddock roe, not often seen in our fishmongers, is prized in France.

HADDOCK

This is the northerner's cod, and in Scotland, north Wales and northern England, haddock is much the more popular fish. I prefer it, because of its oceany flavour.

Another fish of cold waters, it is generally a little smaller than cod and is easily recognised by the dark line down its body and the 'thumbprint' spots on either side — the marks

steaks which you can bake, braise, grill, poach, stir- or shallow-fry, deep-fry or microwave. Whole small cod, called codling, are occasionally available — anything over 14in (30cm) — which you can bake whole and serve for several people. Frozen fillets and fish portions are also widely available. Fresh cod is at its very best June–February.

Cod flesh cooks to a pure snow-white colour; it will flake into plump, moist petals and has a wonderfully gentle flavour. There was a time when people were a bit dismissive of it — not any more, perhaps because it went up in price which encouraged people to cook it more carefully and not let it dry out.

made by St Peter's thumb and finger, according to tradition. Most of our haddock is caught in the North Sea and off the west coast of Scotland and landed at ports such as Fraserburgh, Peterhead and Aberdeen.

Haddock is at its best May–February; you will find it as fresh fillets, cutlets or steaks in the fishmonger and as frozen fillets and fish 'portions' in the supermarket. You may also possibly come across small whole haddock, which are good stuffed and baked whole to serve several people. Try giving it a crunchy gratin coating of breadcrumbs, herbs and cheese.

The flesh of haddock is a little less delicate, more meaty, than cod but can be used in all the same ways — baked, braised, grilled, poached, stir-fried, shallow-fried, deep-fried, steamed or microwaved.

HAKE AND WHITING

HAKE

This silvery-grey relative of the cod is generally a little smaller with a long streamlined body. British fishermen mainly catch it off the north and west coast and land it at ports such as Newlyn, Milford Haven and Ayr. Fleetwood hake was once popular and very plentiful in northern markets and fishmongers, and hake and chips were top of many Lancashire chip shop menus. But since supplies have become scarce the price has risen dramatically (the

Spanish adore hake and are prepared to pay high prices for it) you may not always find it in your local market or supermarket. Much less bony than cod, and more delicate, it is worth seeking out for a treat. You can buy hake whole, or in fillets, cutlets or steaks — it is at its best June–March. It is good baked, braised, grilled, poached, stir- or shallow-fried, steamed or microwaved, but cook it carefully to preserve the flavour and texture.

WHITING

Victorian cookery books are full of dishes for invalids, and recipes for whiting always figure heavily among them. It is by reputation the most digestible fish, and certainly its light texture and flavour make it good for faddy eaters. Some cookery writers are a bit sniffy about it — it does need to be cooked carefully if it isn't going to be dull.

Rounder than hake and generally rather smaller, whiting usually grow to about 15in (38cm) though sometimes you will find bigger specimens. They are mainly trawled in the North Sea and off the Scottish and Irish coast, and Sunday anglers often catch them from the ends of piers.

Whiting is plentiful, always cheap, and at its prime June–February; buy whole fresh fish or fillets, or frozen fillets from the supermarket. Mrs Beeton suggests curling the fish round with their tails in their mouths (a similar traditional Scottish recipe is called Curled Whiting), then

Above: Whiting. *Fish supplied by Tesco. Food Features*

baking them whole, dotted with butter and sweet herbs. I would add seasoning, and 2–3tbsp/40–75ml white wine or fish stock, and seal the ovenproof dish with foil, to keep the fish succulent.

Whiting are also good stuffed and baked; or the fillets can be spread with herby stuffing, rolled up tightly into 'pinwheels' and packed in an ovenproof dish to bake. The fish can also be braised, deep-fried, grilled, poached, stir-fried, steamed or microwaved, but make sure you keep it moist, and help the flavour along with herbs and seasoning.

COLEY, POLLACK AND LING

COLEY

The fishing industry calls it saithe which is also its Scottish name (possibly from the Gaelic *sioghean*). It is also called coalfish because of its

Above: Coley. *Fish supplied by Tesco. Food Features*

dusky colour, and cuddy in the northwest Highlands, but most people know it as coley.

This fish was once important to the people of the Hebrides — the oil was used in lamps, the flesh eaten fresh and dried for winter. And the young fish (pilltocks) were a useful spring catch for Shetland crofters, who caught them using bamboo wands, and seagull feathers or polar bear hairs as flies.

Coley grow up to 40–47in (1–1.2m) and are found all around the coast of Britain, and throughout the eastern Atlantic. They are one of Britain's most important catches, mostly from the North Sea and western Scotland.

This fish has darker flesh than cod, although it whitens during cooking. The skin is very tough and best removed before cooking (except when poaching). Fresh coley is at its peak August–February — you will find it sold as fillets, but also sometimes as cutlets and steaks. Frozen fillets and fish 'portions' are available in supermarkets.

Coley can be used in all the same ways as cod and haddock; some cooks think it is only good for pies and fishcakes, which is a shame; I like to enjoy its meatiness by eating it undisguised.

POLLACK

Sometimes known as lythe, or green cod because of its greenish colour, the pollack grows to 32–40in (80–100cm). It is caught, along with cod, in the North Sea, and in the eastern Atlantic.

Fresh pollack is at its best May–September — it is usually sold as fillets, and sometimes cutlets or steaks, but it is not a very common fish and supplies are unpredictable. It is usually quite inexpensive and the flavour is good, but the flesh can be a bit dry, so cook it with extra moisture. It is useful for made-up dishes such as croquettes and fishcakes — use it like cod or coley.

LING

This is the the giant of the cod family, growing up to 6ft 6in (2m) in length. It has a barbel on its chin and an attractive bronze sheen to its long, mottled body. It is found mainly on the west coast in British waters, and in the Norwegian Sea.

Ling was enjoyed in medieval times, although sometimes confused with cod. 'Ling...being counted the beefe of the sea...yet it is nothing but long cod' sniffed one observer, who then went on to say that it was very good salted and golden yellow (with saffron).

This fish has traditionally been popular in Scotland. In Morayshire, it was served boiled (for that read poached, fish should *never* actually be boiled) with a sauce of dry mustard stirred into melted butter.

You may find fresh ling in the fishmonger's, as fillets or cutlets (it is at its best September–July) though much is salted and whisked away for export, and supplies are unpredictable. Like coley, it has a good solid texture and is inexpensive; use it in the same way.

THE ANCIENT ART OF COOKING STOCKFISH

Stockfish is dried and salted ling or cod, or sometimes other white fish. It was once an important food during the many fasting or 'fish' days imposed by the Church. It is still a part of other national cuisines so you can track it down today in specialist grocers.

The key to successful stockfish preparation is first to make it edible — when you buy it, it can be as hard as a board and is very salty. Medieval cooks hammered, pummelled and soaked it, then often put it into 'Lenten' pies with fruit and spices. Parsnips, used in this recipe, are a traditional partner; their sweetness provides a good foil to the salt:

1 large piece salted ling or other salted white fish
2 onions, sliced
1 onion stuck with cloves
2 parsnips, cut into sticks

1½ pints/850ml milk
freshly ground black pepper
fresh parsley, to garnish

• Soak the fish overnight in cold water (in days gone by it was pegged out in a stream). Discard water and rinse fish.
• Place fish in saucepan with enough fresh water to cover. Bring slowly to boil, then simmer very gently for 10 minutes. Discard water.
• Add milk, onions, parsnips and seasoning to saucepan; bring to boil; simmer very gently until fish is tender.
• Serve garnished with parsley. Traditionally, in Scotland and the North Country this dish was enriched and thickened with egg yolks.

HUSS AND SHARK

HUSS

This was once a fish with a marketing problem: it was known as dogfish, had an unprepossessing appearance and nobody wanted to buy it. Then marketing people devised a new name, 'flake' and, apparently, the fish's fortunes turned. I have never heard it referred to as flake, always huss, or occasionally rigg or rock salmon, though the industry still calls it dogfish. (When presented with the same problem in the USA, a marketing team came up with the infelicitous name of grey-fish. I do not know how well it sells over there.)

The term huss covers a number of

Above: Spinous shark caught off the west of Ireland, a 19th-century illustration. *Town Docks Museum, Hull*

different species of what are in fact small shark caught in British waters. It is plentiful, and is landed in ports all around Britain. Normally the fish are skinned and headed at the port of landing so it is not possible to identify them on the slab (the skin is so rough and tough that it has been used to polish wood, alabaster and copper). Huss is available all year round, sold as fillets or cutlets, though you might not find it in northern mongers.

This is a cartilaginous fish — there are no real bones, and the flesh lifts neatly away when cooked. It has a soft but meaty texture, so is ideal for unreconstructed meat eaters and children, who are bothered by fiddly bones. It can be baked, braised, deep-fried (it is a popular chip shop fish in southern Britain) grilled, poached or shallow-fried. As it holds together well, it is also excellent for stir-frying and for threading on kebabs. It makes an economical substitute for monkfish recipes.

SHARK

This sounds exotic, but for centuries shark have been caught off the British coast — in the Orkneys it was dried for eating in winter.

It is the porbeagle, or mackerel shark, that is usually sold in fishmongers in Britain, or sometimes tope. The porbeagle is found in colder waters than other sharks; it is a fast swimmer which makes its living hunting shoals of herring and mackerel.

Below: Tope. *Food Features*

The porbeagle grows to about 10ft (3m) in length, so you are unlikely to see it whole in the shop; more usually it is sold as steaks or cutlets or long fillets. It is available all year round. The flesh is firm, meaty and filling, and is often compared to veal. The fillets can be sliced into escalopes, and cooked like veal, too. Fresh shark and huss can have an ammoniacal smell, which disappears on cooking.

MONKFISH

This fish is extraordinarily grotesque with its huge mouth, uneven, curving teeth, little eyes on the top of its head, and all kinds of lumps and prickles and protuberances over its body.

Monkfish are fished in the Atlantic, the English Channel and some in the North Sea, as well as the Mediterranean. Peterhead and Newlyn are landing ports. The monkfish lives, often half buried, in the sandy, muddy bottom of the ocean or in seaweedy crevices. It uses its great jaws to swallow up small conger eel, gurnard, haddock, diving seabirds and, according to one source, even lumps of wood.

Also known as the frogmouth, its other name is the angler fish, because of its habit of luring prey by lying motionless and twitching the ray which dangles on top of its head. Inquisitive victims approaching to investigate are snapped up by the angler whose inward-pointing teeth prevent escape.

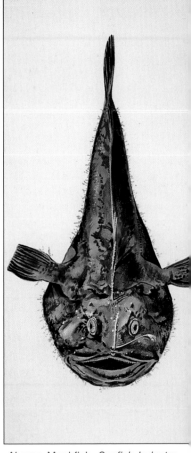

Above: Monkfish. *Seafish Industry Authority*

Monkfish can grow up to 6ft (1.9m) but you will only see much smaller specimens in the shops. Fishmongers usually present the fish ready headed and skinned, or as fillets, in deference to customers' finer feelings.

Not long ago, this fish was of no

economic importance at all, although in some countries the liver was a delicacy. Then someone discovered that monkfish had a flavour and texture like scampi, and it soon became popular; in fact it was sometimes breaded and sold as scampi by unscrupulous merchants. It is now widely available fresh from fishmongers and market stalls throughout the year, but steel yourself before looking at the price tag. When you consider how little fish is left once the giant head is removed, no wonder this is a luxury fish.

Monkfish is very versatile — you can bake, braise, deep-fry shallow-fry, steam, grill, poach or microwave it. The firm flesh holds together and is ideal for barbecuing, stir-frying and stringing on kebabs. Alternatively, a thick fillet of monkfish can be thinly sliced into escalopes which are spread with stuffing, rolled up into pinwheels and baked.

Monkfish tail can also be roasted with garlic, lemon, olive oil, rosemary, crushed bay leaf, salt and pepper; some people say this is very like leg of lamb. Marinate the fish for 1hr in the oil, lemon, herbs and garlic, then roast in the oven, basting regularly.

CATFISH

This peculiar, blunt-nosed fish is also called the wolf-fish, presumably because of its impressive set of canine-like teeth.

It is found all around the British coast, in the North Sea and off Scandinavia, Iceland and Greenland, where it lives at the bottom of the sea and usually grows to 24–40in (60–100cm). Because of its disconcerting appearance, it is almost always skinned and headed before appearing on the fishmonger's slab. Not all markets and fishmongers stock it, but you are most likely to find it sold as fillets. You may also come across it frozen. Fresh catfish is in season February–July.

This is another useful firm-fleshed fish, suitable for baking, braising, deep-frying, grilling, poaching, shallow- or stir-frying, steaming or microwaving. It holds together well if marinated then barbecued and it makes a good fish for pies: along the north Yorkshire and Northumberland coast, it is traditionally made into woof (wolf) pie — the seasoned fish fillets are layered with streaky bacon, hardboiled egg and leek, then topped with shortcrust pastry.

Dorothy Hartley (*Food in England*, 1954) is very scornful of catfish but I think she does the species an injustice; it is a perfectly respectable meaty fish, sometimes found on chip shop menus as rock salmon. Don't confuse it with American catfish, an imported freshwater species and a delicacy in its own right.

JOHN DORY

John Dory probably acquired its unusual name from the Italian term for the fish, janitore, or janitor. It is

Above: John Dory. *Seafish Industry Authority*

sometimes called just dory.

This fish has a distinctive appearance, with a round, compact body when viewed from the side, but so thin when seen straight on that some cookbooks group it with the flat-fish. Its great protruding jaw, which gives it such a comically lugubrious expression, has a purpose: it is hinged so the fish can swing it forward to snatch up its prey — pilchards, sprats and sand smelts. The fish's most marked feature is the big black spot on each of its sides. According to legend, St Peter once drew a gold coin from the mouth of a John Dory and for ever after, all of its kind bore the print of the apostle's finger and thumb, circled with gold. The John Dory was also sacred to Zeus, hence its Latin name *Zeus faber*.

John Dorys are found all around the British coast, and are commonly caught in West Country waters; they are often trawled from sandy grounds. Susan Hicks says that in the Scillies fishermen call them 'handbags', because that is the best way to hold them, by their handle-like ridge on top, to avoid the vicious spines.

John Dorys rarely grow above 16–20in (40–50cm) — you are more likely to come across smallish specimens. Small landings make it an expensive fish, but it is available all year either whole or as quarter-cut fillets. If you are buying and cooking it whole, use a sturdy pair of scissors to snip off the spines.

The flavour of John Dory is superb, sometimes compared to that of turbot, though not as rich. This is one fish best eaten a couple of days after landing, which gives the flesh time to relax and tenderise — consult your fishmonger.

John Dory can be baked, braised, deep-fried, grilled, poached, stir- or shallow-fried, steamed or microwaved. If buying whole, remember to allow for a lot of waste, because of the size of the head. Once the head is removed, you are left with a generous pocket, ideal for stuffing and baking.

CONGER EEL

This great saltwater eel can grow up to 8ft (2.4m). It is a powerful swimmer, found mainly in rocky coastal waters, where it lurks in crevices and old wrecks during the day, coming out at night to feed. It is

Above: Conger Eel. *Fish supplied by Tesco. Food Features*

a voracious predator with needle-like teeth, as some fishermen will tell from painful experience. Congers are a nuisance to coastal fishermen, often raiding their nets and getting into lobster pots. They are, of course, caught in their own right throughout British waters. Alan Davidson describes how the quarrymen of Llanddulas in North Wales catch conger from the water's edge using hooked iron rods to prise them out from under rocks.

Salted dried conger is traditional in the Channel Islands, and in medieval times, congers were split, then rolled up into fat joints and soused in spiced pickle.

You may see a whole conger in the fishmonger, coiled about the fillets and cutlets as an eye-catching display. You won't, of course, want to buy the whole thing. It is normally sold as cutlets or steaks, but you could specially ask for a longer middle cut if you want to stuff and roast it (roast conger was once a favourite food of Cornish tin miners): use a robust-flavoured stuffing, tie up the joint before cooking, and baste well with butter and cider, or wine, while it cooks; the cider helps to break down the gelatinous texture.

Conger is in season March–October. Apart from roasting, you can also bake it with a gratin topping, braise, grill, poach, steam, shallow-fry or microwave it. It has a good flavour and a close texture which does not flake apart so is suitable for stir-frying. I avoid very small conger pieces because of the myriad tiny bones, though they can be used for soup.

GURNARD

The gurnard — or gurnet as it is sometimes called — has a tapering body and a large wedge-shaped armoured head with feeler rays beneath its chin. These rays have tastebuds on them, and the fish uses them to search the bottom of the ocean for food.

There are various species of gurnard, but the most popular in Britain is the red gurnard, also occasionally called the sea cuckoo. The grey gurnard is eaten too, and a

the North Sea. Gurnard are caught by trawl and long line. You will find them fresh at the fishmongers, as whole fish. Gurnard are at their best July–February. Remember when buying to allow for the wastage of the large head, and do not confuse red gurnard with red

Above: Red Gurnard.
Food Features

Scottish name for this fish is crooner because, like all gurnard, it has the odd characteristic that it can croak; gurnard have special muscles in their swimbladders to enable them to do this.

Gurnard typically grow to about 8–12in (20–30cm) but they can be larger. The grey is most common in British waters, the red less often seen in

mullet, a completely different fish, although it looks superficially similar.

Gurnard is well flavoured with firm, white flesh. It is not naturally moist so allow for this when cooking. It can be deep-fried, poached,

braised, stir-fried or shallow-fried in egg and bread-crumbs or a thin batter, micro-waved, or steamed. It is good baked whole with an interesting stuffing; some extra fat in the stuffing will help keep the flesh moist; and baste regularly during cooking with butter or olive oil, or cover with strips of bacon. If you remove the head with the fins and tail before cooking, you can use them to make a sauce or stock for the pan. Gurnard makes excellent soup.

RED MULLET AND GREY MULLET

RED MULLET

This pretty rosy-red fish is a member of a large tropical family, the only member to be found in our waters. The deeper the water where the mullet lives, the richer its colour, which also darkens in the daytime and lightens at night, and according to the fish's emotions.

Red mullet are found along coastlines throughout the eastern Atlantic and the Mediterranean, but not in northern waters where it is too cold. They live on rocky or sandy bottoms, sensing out small prey with their delicate barbels. Red mullet were once a speciality of Weymouth and Portland in Dorset and are still landed in Devon and Cornwall in the

GREY MULLET WITH BLACKBERRY SAUCE

Fruit sauces are traditional accompaniments to fish; the acidity helps to balance the richness of oily fish, while a fruity sweetness combines well with more delicate white fish. Barberries and Seville oranges were favourite choices in the 17th century.

Here, tart apples and blackberries provide a good foil to the substantial meatiness of grey mullet.

2 grey mullet, each 1lb/450gm (or 1 large one) scaled and cleaned
1oz/25gm butter
1 onion, chopped
2 sticks celery, chopped
6oz/175gm cooked brown rice
8oz/225gm cooking apples, cored and diced
2 tsp/10ml ground cinnamon
8oz/225gm blackberries
salt and freshly ground black pepper
¼ pint/150ml water
1oz/25gm soft brown sugar

- Preheat oven, 350°F/180°C/gas 4.
- Melt butter in pan and sauté onion and celery. Remove from heat and stir in rice, apples, 1 tsp/5ml cinnamon, 4oz/110gm blackberries and seasoning.
- Fill mullet with rice mixture and place in covered ovenproof dish. Bake 35–40min, basting occasionally.
- To make sauce: place rest of blackberries and water in pan, cover and cook till fruit is soft.
- Sieve blackberries, stir in sugar and remaining cinnamon. Return to heat and cook till sugar dissolves.

summer months.

These fish were highly valued in classical Roman times for their glittering colour and exquisite flavour — the Roman cookery writer Apicius, writing in the fourth and early fifth century AD, gives several recipes for them, and no doubt Romano-Britons also enjoyed them.

Red mullet is sometimes called the woodcock of the sea, because of

Above: Grey Mullet. *Fish supplied by Tesco. Food Features*

its gamey taste — produced when the liver (a delicacy) and sometimes the rest of the insides are left intact when the fish is cooked.

Red mullet are normally quite small, up to 16in (40cm); you will find them available May–November. They can be cooked whole, or larger fish may be filleted.

The flesh of red mullet is firm and white and quite substantial: some cookbooks class it as an oily fish. You can bake, braise, poach, steam, microwave or shallow-fry it. Small red mullets are excellent grilled with a drizzle of olive oil and some fennel, or baked with fennel, parsley, lemon juice, a little white wine and some butter or olive oil to baste.

GREY MULLET

This handsome silvery-grey fish belongs to a completely different family from that of the red mullet.

Grey mullet live in shoals, in inshore coastal waters, especially estuaries and lagoons. They like soft-bottomed weedy waters which they can sift through for plankton and other tiny animal and plant food. This is what gives them the undeserved reputation for being muddy fish with a muddy taste. Grey mullet are delicious with a good, robust flavour and meaty texture, not too bony and much underrated.

Fresh grey mullet is in season September–February. You will find whole fish of up to 16–24in (40–60cm) in the fishmonger. You could ask your fishmonger to fillet it for you and remember to ask for it to be scaled if you do not want to do it yourself. The fish can be grilled, poached, baked, steamed, microwaved, shallow- or stir-fried. It is excellent stuffed and braised — after stuffing, try wrapping the whole

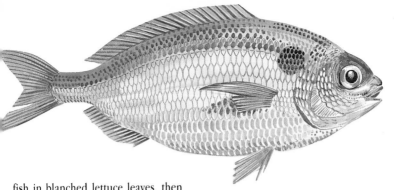

Above: Red Sea Bream
Seafish Industry Authority

fish in blanched lettuce leaves, then dotting with butter and gently braising in cider. I cooked a 3½lb (1.5kg) grey mullet for four people in this way, based on a recipe by Susan Hicks — it sliced very prettily into green-edged portions.

SEA BREAM

These are fish mainly of the warmer waters of the world; they are very abundant in the Mediterranean, and in North America they are known as porgies. There are more than 200 different species in all, but only the red sea bream and the black sea bream are common enough in cooler British seas to be economically important.

Red sea bream are attractive rosy-tinted fish, and larger specimens have a distinctive black spot just behind the gills. They grow up to 14in (35cm), occasionally 20in (50cm).

Red sea bream swim in large shoals in coastal waters and younger specimens can be found in shallow rocky areas and around old wrecks. They are in season June–February.

The black sea bream, also sometimes called old wife, has a more compact, rounder shape than the red bream, when viewed side on. It is an attractive dark slaty-grey colour, grows up to 16–20in (40–50cm) and is often fished from rocky areas and around wrecks. It is in season July–December, and although some people say it is not as good as red bream, I think it is an excellent fish.

In Mrs Beeton's day bream were very common summer visitors to Cornish waters and frequently sold from Hastings fish market, though not very highly thought of. One old recipe suggests that the fish should be cleaned but none of the scales removed. It should then be grilled, turning frequently and dusted with flour if the skin cracks. When the fish is baked, the crispy skin and scales can be peeled away to reveal beautifully moist fish inside, cooked in its own juices. This seems a good way of barbecuing too. Alternatively, the fish can be braised, poached, steamed, stir- or shallow-fried or microwaved.

Sea bream has a good rich flavour and texture, and makes an economical substitute for sea bass. Small fish can be quite fiddly, so if cooking them whole, lift the flesh very carefully away from the bones, or prepare fillets before cooking.

SEA BASS

Sea bass are handsome fish, silvery in colour with a streamlined shape and distinctive black markings on their gills. They are found swimming in small shoals in rocky coastal waters and estuaries. They are ferocious predators with huge appetites for herring and other small shoaling fish, hence their French name, *loup de mer* (sea wolf).

Sea bass are caught all around the British coast, some with rod and line from small boats using prawns as bait. They are popular sporting fish for Sunday anglers. Sea bass are slow-growing, rarely getting larger than 32in (80cm), and because of this, and their increasing scarcity, they can be expensive.

They are considered one of the most delicious fish. In recent years, sea bass has become very fashionable — chefs love to cook it and restaurants like to serve it. It has beautiful white flesh, which is very lean and can be prepared in much the same way as salmon. Perhaps this is why it is sometimes called salmon bass, although it does not belong to the salmon family.

Sea bass are in season August–March. They are excellent baked or braised whole with a flavoursome stuffing. After scaling, rub the fish well with olive oil, or dot with butter. Sea bass steaks or fillets are also good grilled (keep them on the skin, marinate them in lemon juice and olive oil, and baste well to prevent the fish drying out).

Many recipes, inspired by classic Chinese cuisine, combine sea bass with ginger. Try this partnership by adding freshly grated root ginger to a stuffing or marinade. Sea bass can also be grilled, poached, stir-fried, steamed or microwaved.

FLAT-FISH

PLAICE AND SKATE

PLAICE

This is Britain's favourite flat-fish — as much plaice is landed each year in the UK as all other varieties of flat-fish put together.

Plaice are common in the North Atlantic, ranging from the western Mediterranean up as far north as Iceland and Norway, although most British landings come from the North Sea and English Channel. They live on muddy and sandy grounds — according to some, the best come from sandy seas.

Plaice grow to about 35in (90cm) though smaller specimens are often landed. They are right-facing flat-fish, with brown bodies and the familiar bright orange or red spots.

In Denmark and Sweden, plaice is highly prized, but in Britain we tend to think of it as an everyday fish. Mrs Beeton dismisses it as a low-price fish, generally bought by the poor. In her day, the best were reputed to come from the Dowers, or flats between Hastings and Folkestone. Even in medieval times the south coast was known for its plaice fishing — Winchelsea was then an important landing port for the fish, which was often eaten, as today, fried with a garnish of parsley.

Fresh plaice cooked carefully can be excellent, delicate and milky in flavour, though the flavour does vary. It is in season May–February when you will find small whole specimens, or dark- and light- skinned fillets. When you buy a plaice, you might like to ask the fishmonger to remove the tough dark skin as this is quite hard to do. Frozen plaice fillets are also available from supermarkets.

Serve small plaice on the bone, fried in breadcrumbs or they are excellent grilled with lemon, butter and fennel. Plaice can also be steamed or microwaved. Medium-sized whole fish are good boned (ask your fishmonger to do this if necessary) then stuffed and baked, or you can stuff and roll fillets. One 18th-century recipe suggests baking

Below: Plaice.
Food Features

Above: Skate. *Fish supplied by Tesco. Food Features*

the fish with nutmeg, parsley, seasoning, butter, breadcrumbs and a gill (a large splosh) of red wine.

SKATE

This is a most peculiar looking creature; it is almost flat, rectangular in shape with great 'wings' on each side of its body, with which it undulates through the water. Various species of skate and ray are fished, but the industry rarely distinguishes between them and the names are often used interchangeably (sometimes the larger ones are called skate, the smaller rays). All of them are cartilaginous, so have no real bones.

Skate grow up to 5ft (1.5m). They are common bottom-living fish, living on sand and mud and feeding on smaller fish and crustaceans. Most British landings are from the North Sea.

You will probably only come across skate 'wings' in the fishmonger; occasionally the tail or other parts are also used, but they are not very meaty. Skate is in season May-February. Skate has a dry texture and creamy flavour. It is a fish that is best when kept for a day or two after landing because, like shark and huss, it may be quite ammoniacal smelling and tough when very fresh. This is part of a natural process, and the smell disappears after a day or two (any residual ammonia

Skate can be fried, poached in wine or stock, braised, microwaved, baked or grilled. Make sure it does not dry out during cooking. Here, skate wing has been shallow-fried, served with almonds and apple.
Seafish Industry Authority

butter, using capers, parsley and lemon juice. The flesh lifts easily away from the wing once cooked, so this makes an easy fish for children or people anxious about bones.

disappears on cooking) and the flesh becomes quite tender. At one time in Scotland, the fish was put on the grass and covered with sods for a couple of days to allow it to soften, which no doubt worked reasonably well. Obviously no fish should be kept for too long, and by the time it reaches the slab, your skate may well already be a couple of days old, so consult your fishmonger.

A traditional Scottish soup recipe combines skate with onion, herbs and potatoes — a good way to use up the less meaty parts if you see them in the fishmonger. Skate also makes good fishcakes but the traditional accompaniment to skate wings is black

FLOUNDER, WITCH AND DAB

FLOUNDER

The flounder is a close relative of the plaice, and fishermen sometimes land hybrids where the two species spawn together. Unlike plaice, flounders rarely get bigger than 20in (50cm). Brownish-green in colour with dull orange spots, they are found in coastal waters and estuaries, but are also in deeper Atlantic waters. They also seem to be quite tolerant of freshwater — they have been kept in ponds, and have been found swimming in the Thames as far

Above: Flounder. *Food Features*

up as Teddington in Middlesex. In the 19th century, Thames flounder were deemed a delicate fish.

Flounder is not particularly popular in Britain today, and is generally thought inferior to plaice. Like plaice it does vary in quality.

It is in season March–November. You can use it whole or as fillets, in all the same ways as plaice — baked, braised, grilled, egg and breadcrumbed then fried, steamed, or microwaved. Serve it with an interesting pouring sauce if you are worried it might be dull.

WITCH

Another relative of the plaice, witch is sometimes called witch flounder, sometimes pole dab, fluke or Torbay sole. It is found on muddy seabeds in the North Atlantic, and in British waters especially in the northern North Sea, off the Scottish and northwest coast.

Witch is sometimes a little bigger than flounder, 22–24in (55–60cm), greyish-brown, with a more elongated shape. It is recognisable by its raggedy-looking fins. Don't confuse it with sole which has a similar shape.

Witch has a good flavour, but is not a fish everyone enthuses about, probably because of all the bones: it is rather thin with a low yield of flesh. Witch is in season May–February and can be used in

Opposite:
A sailing trawler catching turbot and other flat-fish, 1888. The rope at the mouth of the beam trawl was weighted with chain so that it scraped along the seabed, disturbing the fish which rose off the bottom and into the net. This same principle is used with modern trawl nets. *Town Docks Museum, Hull*

much the same ways as plaice.

DAB

This little relative of the plaice and flounder rarely gets bigger than 10in (25cm). It is one of the most common flat-fishes of the northeastern Atlantic and the North Sea where it likes to live on sandy shoals and banks. It is abundant in shallow inshore waters — David Mabey (*In Search of Food*, 1978) enjoyed freshly-caught dab straight from the water and fried in a pan of butter; he describes dab-spearing from the shore near Stiffkey in Norfolk, using bamboo poles as spears.

Dabs are a yellowish colour often freckled and speckled with brown and orange. They are in season September–May, and are an economical fish with a good flavour and firm texture. Small ones can be fried whole as David Mabey enjoyed them (skin them first if you like) or baked, grilled, poached or microwaved.

TURBOT, BRILL AND MEGRIM

TURBOT

This is the aristocrat of the flat-fishes; its flavour is exquisite, and its price generally reflects its reputation. The Romans called it the pheasant of the sea, but an old Scottish name is bannock-fluke, because it is round and flat like an oaten bannock.

Unlike the plaice family which are

TRAWL BEAM FISHING GEAR

Above: Turbot *and (top) Brill. Fish supplied by Tesco. Food Features*

right-facing flat-fish (see p 37), the turbot is generally left-facing. It can sometimes grow up to 40in (1m) in size, and is a thick fish.

Turbot are found in inshore waters around Europe from Norway to the Mediterranean, and in the North Sea. They live on shelly, sandy, or rocky seabeds, their skin colour varying from light grey-brown to deep chocolate colour with green spots. The turbot has no scales, but little bony knobs, or tubercles, on its skin.

In medieval times, turbot was eaten with green herb sauce, or sometimes made into a cold fish jelly, spiced and coloured with saffron for a special feast. Mrs Beeton suggests cooking turbot whole ('1 middling-sized turbot for 8 persons') in a proper turbot-kettle, which is rounder and shallower than normal fish kettles 'thus exactly answering to the shape of the fish'. She also warns readers not to cut off the fins, which are a delicacy.

These days you will find large turbot sold in fillets or steaks; or you may find whole little 'chicken turbot'. It is in season April–February.

Firm textured and fine flavoured, turbot does not need to be smothered by strong-flavoured sauces or dressings: bake, braise, shallow- or stir-fry, grill, steam, poach or microwave it. Lobster sauce is a traditional accompaniment.

BRILL

From the same family as the turbot, brill grow to 12–24in (30–60cm). The brill's skin is smooth, without the little bony knobs of the turbot.

These fish are found in shallow water on sandy, muddy or gravelly grounds. They can also live in brackish water, and are fished all around the British coastline. Some are landed in Scotland and Northern Ireland, but most come into English and Welsh ports.

Brill are thinner than turbot, but have excellent flavour. Perhaps because they don't carry the same weighty reputation, they are usually less expensive. They can be cooked in all the same ways. You will find them in season June–February.

MEGRIM

This is another relative of the turbot, a poor relation perhaps, but quite good if jumped up with an interesting sauce or marinade.

Sometimes called whiff, meg and even, rather optimistically, Scarborough sole, megrim has yet another name, sail-fluke. This, says

Above: Turbot. Seafish Industry Authority

Alan Davidson, derives from Orkney where it was once believed the fish could up-end itself with its tail poking out of the water which it then used as a sail!

Megrim are sandy-brown in colour with darker blotches, oval in shape, and rarely bigger than 20in (50cm). They are not usually found in shallow coastal waters; British trawlers mostly catch them in the north, west, and southwest.

Megrim are in season May–March. They can be used whole, or a large fish can be filleted. Bake, braise, fry, grill, poach, steam or microwave them. The flesh can be dry, so be sure to baste well if baking or grilling. Consider giving this fish some extra flavour with a spicy sauce, a piquant marinade or a rich, cheesy topping.

HALIBUT

This is the giant of the flat-fishes — leviathans of 10–13ft (3–4m) have

Above: Halibut. *Food Features*

been caught in the past, although today specimens over 6ft 6in (2m) are very rare. Halibut have long oval bodies, olive-green backs and pearly white undersides, though colours do vary.

These are fish of northern waters, often caught along with cod, although they are also fished for in their own right, and make small, but valuable landings for northeastern ports such as Hull and Fraserburgh. They are mainly deep-water fish.

In 1987, the British Halibut Association was set up in Argyll to develop the possibilities of halibut farming. Trials have gone well, apparently, and the Association predicts that farmed Atlantic halibut will be in the shops by 1996. Hopefully, this will mean lower prices for this delicious fish.

Today, halibut is highly regarded, but in the early 19th century nobody wanted to eat it. Catches often went for fertiliser, and up in the Shetlands the large flat-fish were sometimes laid out on the beach as temporary slipways for hauling up the sixerns — the six-oared cod fishing boats.

Halibut is in season June–March. You will not see whole large fish in the market or fishmonger's; look out for steaks or fillets, or for whole little 'chicken' halibut which can be cooked like sole.

When cooking halibut steaks, make sure you baste the fish well. Try baking well seasoned steaks, basted with butter, and with a generous splash of cider in the bottom of the dish. Halibut is also good braised, which keeps it moist, poached, grilled or microwaved. It is firm-textured, so suitable for stir-frying. In Iceland it is made into a soup with prunes or rhubarb.

DOVER SOLE AND LEMON SOLE

DOVER SOLE

The name of this fish comes from the Ancient Greeks' word for sandal presumably because of its sandal shape. In Britain we call it Dover sole because that was the port that traditionally served London, although Mrs Beeton thought the best soles came from Torbay (but don't confuse this fish with witch, which is sometimes called Torbay sole.)

Many people consider Dover sole the best of all flat-fish, and because of this it has been the subject of astonishingly rich and elaborate dishes in the past. Food fashions change, however, and these days most people like to cook it very simply indeed; after all, what is the point of swamping the delectable

Above: Lemon Sole and (top) Dover Sole. *Fish supplied by Tesco. Food Features*

flavour with power dressing?

Dover sole normally grow to about 20–24in (50–60cm). They are right-hand facing fish (see p 37), with a dark-brown upper side, and are found from the Mediterranean north to southern Norway, and in the southern North Sea. Brixham, Newlyn, Lowestoft and Fleetwood are all landing ports.

Fresh Dover sole is in season May–February and is available whole, or as fillets of larger fish. (You may see frozen Dover sole, but remember that the flavour will be impaired by freezing.) You can ask the fishmonger to remove the dark skin,

and remember to scale the underside too. Fresh sole is at its best a couple of days after landing, so consult your fishmonger.

Perhaps nothing can improve on Dover soles plainly grilled, basted with butter and served with wedges of lemon; Eliza Acton suggests baking them with a breadcrumb topping seasoned with mace and cayenne and moistened with liquid butter; or they can be flour-dipped, fried and served with a classic frothy golden butter sauce. Alternatively, you could poach, steam or microwave them.

LEMON SOLE

The lemon sole is not really a sole at all; it belongs to the same family as plaice. Its other name is smear dab, and in Scotland it is sometimes just called sole.

Lemon soles are usually about the same size as Dovers, but rounder — more lemon-shaped — and a bright golden or sandy colour. They live on the seabed, on rocky bottoms and are found off Iceland, the Faroes, and Norway, in the North Sea and English Channel and to the west of Britain. About twice as much lemon sole is landed as Dovers, although the catch is not nearly as valuable.

Lemon soles are in season May–March, as fillets or small whole fish. You can ask your fishmonger to remove the upper skin for you. You might also find frozen lemon sole. Lemon sole has excellent flavour, and can be used in much the same way as Dover.

OIL-RICH FISH

MACKEREL

Britain's fishing fleet catches more mackerel than it does any other single species. In medieval times, the fish was cried through the streets of London and, because of its perishability, was even allowed to be sold on Sunday. In the 18th century small mackerel smacks came up the Thames in full sail from Folkestone to ensure the freshness of London's supplies.

The humble mackerel is a beautiful fish, with a long streamlined body, gorgeous iridescent green and blue above with dark stripes, and delicate silvery-white below. Mackerel swim in shoals and in summer feed voraciously: Mrs Beeton retells a gruesome tale by the 17th-century writer Pontoppidan, how a Norwegian sailor 'having gone into the sea to bathe, was suddenly missed by his companions...'. After a

Above: Cider Soused Mackerel.
Seafish Industry Authority

46

few minutes he reappeared some
distance out to sea 'with a great
number of mackerel clinging to him

Above: Mackerel fleet off the coast
of Ireland, a 19th-century
illustration. *Town Docks Museum,
Hull*

SOUSED MACKEREL

Originally, mackerel was soused in spiced vinegar as a way of preserving it,
though Cornish cooks sometimes used a less potent pickle of half vinegar
and half tea or cider. Once cooked, the mackerel would be strained from the
liquor and eaten cold, for tea or breakfast. This recipe is equally good hot or
cold. *Seafish Industry Authority*

2 mackerel, each 1lb/450gm
salt and freshly ground black pepper
juice and thinly pared rind of ½ lemon
1 onion, sliced
sprigs fresh thyme and rosemary
4 fresh bay leaves
½ pint/300ml dry cider
¼ pint/150ml water
1 tsp/5ml arrowroot
fresh herbs, to garnish

- Preheat oven, 325°F/160°C/gas 3.
- Season fish and arrange in ovenproof dish.
  Add lemon rind, onion, herbs and bay leaves.
- Pour cider, lemon juice, and water over fish. Cover with foil and bake,
  30–40min.
  When cooked, strain and transfer fish to serving dish; keep warm.
- Reserve ½ pint/300ml of cooking liquor.
- Blend arrowroot with a little water, then stir into reserved liquor.
- Pour into saucepan.
- Bring to boil, stirring continuously. Simmer till sauce clears.
- Pour over fish and serve immediately.

Above: (left to right) Mackerel, grey mullet and red mullet. *Food Features*

by their mouths. His comrades hastened in a boat to his assistance; but when they had struck the fishes from him...he was so severely bitten, that he shortly afterwards died.'

Mackerel range from the Mediterranean to the North Atlantic: in summer they are fished throughout the waters of Europe's continental shelf, then they move to their overwintering grounds in the northern North Sea and south and west of Britain, moving again in spring to their spawning grounds in the Celtic Sea. Scottish and West Country ports are important landing points. In the Southwest, there is still a handline mackerel fishery.

These are oil-rich fish, which is why they spoil quickly. More than any other fish I know, mackerel is incomparably better when cooked absolutely fresh from the sea.

Mackerel are available all year; you will find them whole in the fishmonger, 12–24in (30–60cm) fish are normal, which you can then bone and fillet if you like. Mackerel can be baked, grilled, barbecued, fried, braised or microwaved. The flesh is very rich, so add any extra fat with discretion, and use vinegar, lemon or other acid fruit to help counteract the oiliness. Gooseberry sauce with mackerel is traditional, a combination reputedly brought over at the time of the Norman Conquest.

HERRING AND PILCHARD

HERRING

Our waters once teemed with herring and whole fishing communities flourished and fell with the vicissitudes of the great seasonal shoal migrations — the Vikings,

The herring is a small streamlined fish, up to 2ft (60cm) long, though you are more likely to see them at about 8–12in (20–30cm) in the shops, a pretty steely-blue or -green colour over their back, and silvery below. Most of our herring these days are caught in the North Sea, Irish Sea and west of Scotland.

Herring are one of our cheapest, most nutritious fish. They are in season May–December, though you can buy them at other times.

according to some historians, invaded Britain partly because they coveted our herring fishery.

By the 1950s overfishing, and maybe a change in migration patterns, created a massive decline in the industry, but from the mid-1970s to the mid-1980s there was a complete ban on fishing North Sea herring and stocks have now regenerated somewhat.

Trawling for herring off the Clyde. Here the catch is being sorted and boxed on board.
Scottish Fisheries Museum, Fife

Aficionados disagree as to when they are at their very best — in spring they are lean and drier, in autumn fatter and richer.

Until I became adventurous with herring recipes, I had no idea how

versatile this fish could be. For people who do not like eating around bones, it is essential to fillet before cooking — not a speedy task, but worth doing (some people recommend using tweezers). You can bake, braise, grill or microwave herring. Horseradish is an excellent accompaniment, and in Wales and northern England apples are used. The traditional way of cooking herring in Scotland is to grill or fry it coated in oatmeal — the oats balance the richness of the fish. Pinhead oatmeal is best, but rolled (porridge) oats make a reasonable substitute.

Keep the roe if you find it in a

herring — it is one of the best parts; soft herring roes can also be bought separately and are delicious dusted with flour and fried or grilled.

STAR-GAZEY AND THE MYSTERY OF THE DISAPPEARING PILCHARD

Pilchards and sardines are exactly the same species — sardines are simply young pilchards. You only occasionally see fresh pilchards in the shops these days, but they were once caught in vast quantities off the Cornish coast and formed a great and profitable industry. 'Huers' were employed to stand on the clifftops and watch for the approach of the shoal. When they saw the tell-tale reddish tinge in the water, they waved as a sign to get ready the boats. Then just before World War 1, the pilchards stopped coming. Nobody knows why, but the whole industry collapsed virtually overnight.

A delightful legacy of the old pilchard fishery and a traditional Cornish dish, star-gazey pie is so called because the fish are arranged around the piedish with their heads poking through the pastry, staring at the stars; that way, the valuable fish oil drained into the pie, and the inedible heads could be removed. If

2 eggs, hardboiled, shelled and sliced
8oz/225gm shortcrust or puff pastry
beaten egg to glaze

• Preheat oven to 400°F/200°C/gas mark 6.
• Mix breadcrumbs, onion, 2 tbsp/40ml parsley, lemon rind and juice, nutmeg and seasoning and use mixture to stuff fish.
• Arrange fish in shallow pie dish with heads sticking up.
• Sprinkle bacon over fish, then arrange egg slices on top and sprinkle on remaining parsley.
• Roll out pastry. Fit pastry lid, pressing it around fishheads. Brush with egg and bake 35– 40min.

Whitebait, deep-fried and garnished with toasted almonds.
Seafish Industry Authority

you have an aversion to beady-eyed fishheads, make the pie with the heads removed.

8–10 pilchards, 12 sardines or 6 small herring cleaned and boned
4oz/110gm fresh wholemeal breadcrumbs
1 onion, finely chopped
6 tbsp/100ml chopped fresh parsley
grated rind and juice ½ lemon
1 tsp/5ml grated nutmeg
salt and freshly ground black pepper
4oz/110gm cooked streaky bacon, chopped

SPRATS AND WHITEBAIT

SPRATS

These small silvery relatives of the herring rarely get bigger than 5½in (14cm). They swim in shoals around coastal areas, sometimes venturing into the brackish waters of estuaries. Garvie is a Scottish name for them.

Sprats have always been plentiful and cheap — pickled sprats were a staple food of the medieval poor. Suffolk, Essex and the Kent coast

Above Sprats. *Fish supplied by Tesco. Food Features*

have been particularly famous for them and in Victorian times 400–500 boats were kept busy catching them through the winter. Aldeburgh was especially noted for its sprats and the season's first catch was traditionally sent to grace the table of the Lord Mayor's banquet in London each year.

Sprats are still plentiful and cheap in season — you might be lucky and be able to buy them fresh from the quayside; alternatively, find them at the fishmonger's or market; make sure they are very bright-eyed. They are in season October–March.

Sprats can be baked, grilled, fried or microwaved. David Mabey describes the Suffolk way of cooking them — putting them whole into a hot frying pan sprinkled with salt. The salt draws out the natural oils in the fish, and they fry in this; no extra fat is needed. You can dust them with fine oatmeal first if you like.

Cook them for 2min each side then eat, holding the head and tail between your fingers. They are also good deep-fried.

WHITEBAIT

This is not a species of fish at all, but the collective term for the small fry of herring and sprats. Tiny silvery fish, no more than 4in (10cm) long, they are bought, cooked and eaten whole — heads, tails and all.

Whitebait are often available frozen these days; or you may find them sold fresh in summer. They are best dipped in milk, then shaken in a paper bag of seasoned flour, and batch-fried in deep oil for a couple of minutes, till crisply golden. The 19th-century way was to devil them by sprinkling cayenne pepper over before serving.

FRESHWATER FISH

SALMON AND SEA TROUT

SALMON

The Atlantic salmon is a fish with an extraordinary life cycle — it spawns in high gravelly streams; the fry emerge, remain in the river for a couple of years, then travel down to the sea and cross the ocean to feeding grounds in the North Atlantic where they stay for 14 years, before making the great journey back, hundreds of miles to their natal

A KETTLE OF SALMON

Tweed kettle is an old Scottish way of cooking salmon, popular in 19th-century Edinburgh. It gets its name from that great salmon river, the Tweed, and from the fish kettle used to cook the fish. The salmon was simmered for 1 minute, then skinned, boned and cut into pieces. The skin and bones were added to the liquor and simmered to make fish stock. Wine, shallots, mace and seasoning were added to the strained stock, and the salmon was simmered for a further 3 minutes. Then it was served hot with neeps, mashed potatoes or girdle scones. Gentle poaching is a good way to cook any salmon. In this version, the salmon is kept whole and, because it is to be eaten cold, is simply brought to a simmer then left to sit in the poaching liquor as it cools.   *Scottish Salmon Board*

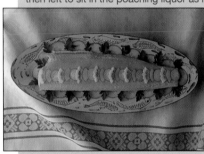

5–7lb/2.25–3kg whole salmon
for the court bouillon:
1 bottle dry white wine (cheap plonk is fine)
2 bay leaves
2 onions, peeled and sliced
2 carrots, sliced
1 celery stick
4 tbsp/75ml white wine vinegar
12 peppercorns
1 tbsp/20ml salt

fresh sprigs parsley or dill, to garnish
lemon and cucumber slices, to decorate

• Place cleaned, gutted salmon (head and tail removed if you prefer) on rack in fish kettle or in large pan.
• Pour over bottle of white wine, topping up with cold water till fish is covered.
• Having measured correct quantity of cooking liquid remove fish, add 2 bay leaves, onions, carrots, celery, wine vinegar, peppercorns and salt.
• Bring to boil across two burners, lower heat and simmer for 20–30min.
• Remove from heat and carefully add fish. Return to heat. As soon as liquid bubbles, turn off heat, cover with close-fitting lid and leave to cool.
• When cool, carefully drain fish and gently remove skin.
• Transfer to serving dish and garnish with parsley or dill sprigs, and alternate cucumber and lemon slices. Serve with new potatoes and tossed green salad.

rivers to spawn. Nobody really knows how they find their way back — some say by smell — but less than one salmon in 1,000 makes a mistake and ends up in the wrong river.

Traditionally, these beautiful silvery fish have been caught by nets and traps at river mouths as they start their journey back upstream, or by rod and line further upriver. Salmon were once plentiful in our waterways, and it is said that they were once so common, that it was fed to servants and apprentices till they were sick of the sight of them. Whether true or not, wild salmon are

grilled, poached, steamed, stir-fried, baked, braised or microwaved — the important thing to remember is not to let it dry out, so baste regularly if grilling or baking. Small or large whole fish, or middle cuts can be stuffed and baked. Salmon tail can be roasted.

SEA TROUT

This is also called salmon trout, and sewin in Wales where it is a great national speciality. When fresh from the sea it is distinguishable from brown (river) trout by its long silvery body (after the fish has entered the

Above: Sea trout and (top) wild salmon. Food Features

Below: A dish of sewin (Welsh sea trout) with wild mushroom sauce at the Lake Hotel, Llangammarch Wells. Welsh Food Promotions

not so abundant now, though small supplies are still available from spring through to summer, or even in autumn from further upstream. This is a very expensive, but delectable, firm, meaty fish.

Supplies of farmed salmon, especially from the lochs of the Western Highlands and Islands, are plentiful; most supermarkets and fishmongers stock it, and the price has tumbled so it is no longer a luxury fish. Farmed salmon is maybe not quite as firm textured as wild, but nevertheless has excellent flavour and is available all year round. Scottish growers operate a quality assurance scheme for their salmon and display an octagonal tartan sticker.

Salmon steaks or cutlets can be

rivers to spawn, its colour changes and identification is less easy). It can look very similar to young salmon, too, but its tail is less bifurcated.

Sea trout are found in fast-flowing, clean rivers, especially in the Western Highlands, the Spey, the Tweed and many Welsh rivers. They spawn in the upper reaches, migrate down to the sea, then return to their spawning ground to breed.

Sea trout, says Simon Newnes of Billingsgate, make even better eating than wild salmon, which is praise indeed. Finer textured than salmon, it can be cooked in the same ways.

BROWN TROUT, RAINBOW TROUT AND CHAR

BROWN TROUT

Britain's native freshwater trout is the brown trout, also called the river trout.

Like many other lads from Welsh mining valleys, my great-grandfather knew the art of tickling trout from the local brook. Today, hotels, inns and country clubs throughout the country maintain trout streams for their angling patrons.

Wild trout come in a variety of shapes, colours, and sizes — some people say these are different races of trout, others say not. In some areas, intermediates between sea and brown trout are found, which are rather unattractively called slob trout; in the deep cold lochs of

northern Scotland and in the Lake District the huge and ugly ferox trout lives and reaches giant proportions.

Today, brown trout are common in streams, rivers and lakes. The game fishing season for brown trout is March–end September. Brook trout is farmed in France, so you may find it in your fishmonger's.

River trout are delicious, although the flavour varies — chalky stream trout are said to have firmer, richer flesh than acid water trout. The flesh is normally white. Most are about 12in (30cm) long and weigh 12–16oz (350–450gm), though larger fish are not uncommon, and if you are ever offered a ferox, you could be dealing with up to 25lb (11.4kg).

Grill, bake, poach, steam, braise, fry or microwave trout. In a traditional Welsh recipe, trout with bacon, the fish are wound in streaky rashers, seasoned well with freshly ground black pepper and baked in a preheated oven for about 20 minutes or shallow-fried in hot oil for 10 minutes each side, till the bacon is crisp.

A Victorian method is to cook cleaned whole trout in newspaper. If you are doubtful about the newspaper ink (it isn't particularly good for you, which is why fish and chips are no longer wrapped in it) beg a few extra sheets of your fishmonger's white wrapping paper. Soak the sheets of paper in water, then wrap around the seasoned fish, smoothing the first layer against the trout, and tucking in the ends. Bake in an oven for about 30 minutes, or

Above: Rainbow Trout. *Fish supplied by Tesco. Food Features*

till the paper is dry. When unwrapped, the innermost layer neatly pulls away the skin, leaving the succulent flesh exposed.

RAINBOW TROUT

This is not a native of Britain, but an American species introduced by fish farmers, and the one you commonly find in fishmongers. It is cheap, plentiful, available all year, and also available frozen.

Most rainbow trout are sold as 12–16oz (350–450gm) fish. Cook them as you would brown trout, perhaps with an interesting stuffing or sauce. A traditional English way with trout is to fry it in butter, then serve topped with toasted split almonds.

CHAR

This is a relative of the trout. In Britain it lives in deep, land-locked lakes — in Wales, in the lochs of Scotland and in the Lake District. As each population of char has been isolated since the last Ice Age many distinct races have evolved.

Lake Windermere char is the most famous. In the 18th century, Windermere potted char became very fashionable — the little fish were thickly encased in butter, sealed in special china char pots (which are now valuable collectors' items) and sent all over the country.

Hybrid char are now farmed in Scotland, but if you want to taste wild Windermere char, you will have to ask a local fisherman, or you may find some for sale in Windermere or Bowness in season. The Rothay Manor Hotel, Ambleside, has traditional potted char on the menu, May–July. Trout could be used as a substitute in this recipe:

ROTHAY MANOR POTTED CHAR

3 cleaned char each about
8–10oz/225–300gm — (about
1lb/450gm cooked fish)
8oz/225gm butter
1/4 pint/150ml cream
salt and freshly ground black pepper
pinch ground nutmeg and mace
2 tsp/10ml dry white wine
2 tsp/10ml lemon juice
For the court bouillon:
4 pints/2.25 litres water
1/2oz/12gm salt
juice of 1 lemon
2–3 sprigs parsley
6 black peppercorns
2oz/50gm carrots
1 bay leaf

- Bring court bouillon ingredients to boil in large pan, then strain.
- Poach char gently in court bouillon for 8–10min. Skin and bone fish.
- Place in food processor, add melted butter, seasonings, lemon juice and wine, and process to a paste.
- Mix in cream.
- Put into ramekin dishes; pour over a little clarified butter and place in fridge to set.   Serve with warm toast fingers.

A haul of bream, caught at Ely in 1911. *Ely Museum*

CARP, BREAM, TENCH AND ROACH

CARP

We have a long history of eating carp in this country, but it isn't a native fish. It was probably introduced in the 14th century and became a favourite species for the stewpond (an artificial pond for breeding fish). Most medieval monasteries kept well-stocked stewponds for the refectory table.

Today we are rather prejudiced about eating any freshwater fish except salmon and trout, which is why carp isn't common in fishmongers, although a certain amount finds its way to cities to supply ethnic populations. *Larousse Gastronomique* gives 19 different ways of cooking it.

Carp are found in slow-moving rivers and ponds. They live to a great age, some say they can reach 150, and can grow enormous. They are farmed in Britain, mainly for restocking lakes, and regularly appear at Billingsgate, so your fishmonger may be able to order you some. There are three varieties — the common carp, the pretty greenish-gold mirror carp and the grass carp.

The best season for carp is November–April. The flesh is firm and white, but it does have quite a few sharp bones. Carp can be braised, poached, fried or grilled.

STUFFED BAKED CARP

Mrs Beeton suggests stuffing carp with a delicate forcemeat (parsley, lemon and well-seasoned breadcrumbs, perhaps). The fish is then egg and breadcrumbed and placed in an ovenproof dish. Drizzle melted butter over the breadcrumbs.

58

Above: Carp. *Fish supplied by Tesco. Food Features*

Add:
½ pint/300ml fish stock (or water)
½ pint/300ml port (or sherry)
6 anchovies
2 onions sliced
1 bay leaf
1 tsp/5ml fresh chopped marjoram
½ tsp/2.5ml castor sugar
salt and cayenne pepper.

• Bake in a moderate oven for 1hr. Use the thickened juices (and some extra lemon juice) to make a pouring sauce.

Carp like to root around in the soft bottoms of waters, and because of this they tend to have an earthy, some say muddy, flavour. This can be improved by the following method: before cooking, wash the cleaned fish thoroughly in running water, then soak for 3–4 hours in a weakish solution of vinegar and water, or in salted water. The method can also be used for tench and roach.

BREAM, TENCH AND ROACH

All these relatives of the carp are found in British waters and are caught by coarse anglers, who usually throw them back. You may come across them in specialist fish shops. Wild roach and bream are fished from Lough Neagh in Ireland and sometimes find their way here. Roach has quite an earthy flavour — you are most likely to find it in cities with Indian communities who know how to cook it. Bream, a beautiful deep-bodied fish, is enjoyed by ethnic communities, and large bream (as well as carp and pike) are made into the famous gefilte fish by Jewish cooks. Some farmed tench from the Netherlands comes to Britain.

PIKE, PERCH AND ZANDER, SHAD AND WHITEFISH

PIKE

This ferocious predator has long shark-like jaws bristling with teeth, a powerful, streamlined body mottled silver and grey and is found in many British waters, from canals to lakes and lochs. It is a solitary hunter, lurking in reeds to ambush its prey, and where food supplies are good it can reach a hefty size.

In medieval times, pike were bred for the table in stewponds — baloc or balourgly broth was a favourite medieval recipe; the pike was cut into pieces and stewed in spiced wine and water.

Pike have delicious white flesh — the very best are the young pickerels. You may not see this fish in your fishmonger, but it is eaten by Jewish communities and is regularly sold at Billingsgate, so your fishmonger may be able to get some.

Izaak Walton (*The Compleat Angler,* 1653) suggests stuffing pike with anchovies, the minced liver, breadcrumbs, butter, herbs and mace, and basting with red wine and garlic before baking. Oranges, more butter and oysters are then added.

Above Pike. *Fish supplied by Tesco. Food Features*

Alternatively, you could fillet the fish to get rid of the bones, or make quenelles (little fish dumplings) from it, which is the classic way with pike.

PERCH AND ZANDER

These belong to the same family but the zander, also called the pike-perch, is not a native and was introduced in the 19th century. They are some of the best freshwater fish for eating,

enter rivers to spawn. This is where they are traditionally caught — shad from the Severn were formerly sold to the mining communities of the Forest of Dean. These days they are sometimes found in estuarine salmon traps, in the River Tweed and Mersey. The adults look similar to herring, but with dark spots near the gills.

Shad has a subtler flavour than herring. Try cooking it as Jane Grigson recommends — wrapped in foil and baked very slowly for 6 hours. This reduces the bones to crunchy edibility.

WHITEFISH

These are a regional speciality — small silvery fish, which look like herring and are found in some of Britain's deepest lakes, where they were probably trapped in the last Ice Age. Different species are found in different lakes: the schelly or gwyniad lives only in Lake Bala in Wales and in the Lake District, the powan is found only in Loch Lomond and Loch Eck, while the little vendace is found in the Lake District and Dumfries and Galloway.

All whitefish make good eating, but they are rare. White-fleshed, firm and quite rich, they can be grilled, baked, or fried.

with firm, white flaky flesh — a bit like John Dory — which is easily lifted from the bones. Some perch and zander are imported from the Netherlands, where they are raised by trout farmers.

Small perch are good fried whole in egg and breadcrumb, or cooked in cider or wine.

SHAD

Shad are members of the herring family, fish of coastal waters which

EELS AND ELVERS

The eel is a remarkable traveller. The tiny larva starts life 2,500 miles (4,000km) away in the middle of the Sargasso Sea and then drifts slowly to

Europe on the Gulf Stream. It reaches the European coast after 2½ years, then metamorphoses into a little transparent elver and swims upriver. There it stays feeding and growing until eventually it turns round and makes the long swim back to the Sargasso Sea.

Most eels are caught by traps, lines and nets as they journey down to the sea, but elvers are also caught in spring going upstream. River Severn elvers are famous. Easter Monday used to be the high point of

Below:

Paul Gotobed in his backyard near Ely, Cambridgeshire, in the 1890s, making a basket eel trap; larger traps, called grigs, stand at the side. The Fens have always been famous for eels and in the Middle Ages, Fenland villages and towns sometimes paid their rents in the form of eel pies, while live eels were regularly carted to London in water butts. Ely's last remaining eel fisherman gave up using basket traps in the 1980s and now uses funnel-shaped, hooped nets. *Ely Museum*

Above: Eels.
Food Features

markets still stock that well-known London delicacy, jellied eels.

Eel and pie shops were once common in London and the Southeast. One of the few survivors is F. Cooke & Sons in the East End. There you can buy hot eels served with steak and kidney pie, mashed potato and parsley sauce to eat in or take away, cold jellied eels, and live or freshly prepared eels to take home.

the Gloucestershire elver season when villages along the Severn, such as Frampton and Epney, held elver-eating contests. Now the elver harvest is one tenth of what it was in the 1970s and live elvers are exported to Europe and Japan for stocking lakes and eel farms, so are rarely available for eating. You may be lucky and find them March–late April at Gloucester market, but be prepared to pay a steep price. In Epney they were always fried in bacon fat, then with beaten egg added to the pan.

Full-grown eels are still caught, especially in East Anglia, the Thames, and the Severn. And fishmongers, and

Eels must be cooked soon after killing, so buying them live was once normal practice. It used to be recommended that you skin the eels alive, which is revolting, and something nobody does now. At reputable fishmongers, the eels are humanely and expertly killed.

Eel pies were at one time another London speciality. They were taken for picnics on the Thames, and eventually gave their name to Eel-Pie Island, near Richmond. Eels can also be stewed, poached or fried.

SHELLFISH
CRUSTACEANS
CRAB

COMMON CRAB

This is also called the brown or edible crab, and in some areas of Scotland the partan, which is just the Gaelic word for crab (crabs were once an important food for the people of the Scottish Highlands and Islands, who used to bait and trap them in deep rockpools on the beaches).

Above: Dressed Crab

Common crabs are found all around the British coast. They are caught in baited pots or creels and are the only crab species of any real commercial importance. Grimsby, Newlyn and Ullapool are all crabbing ports.

North Norfolk is probably the most famous place in Britain for crabs. Blakeney, Sheringham and Cromer are all centres for the coastal crabbing boats, and on a good day, a Cromer fisherman might haul up 700 crabs or more from his pots. Norfolk fishing families usually boil, dress and sell their own catches, and you can see handwritten signs advertising freshly dressed crab all along the coastal roads.

When buying a crab, choose a medium-sized one that is heavy for its size, and make sure there are no cracks in the shell and that you cannot hear water sloshing about inside. The season for common crabs varies around the coast; in Cornwall the potting season is March –November.

Most fresh crab is cooked and picked at the port of landing and fishmongers and supermarkets often sell it ready dressed. Some fishmongers sell boiled crab still in their shells, and will open and prepare them for you, or you can do it yourself. You may also find live crabs for sale (see p 15,DISPATCHING LIVE SHELLFISH HUMANELY). An uncooked crab should be boiled for about 10–12 minutes, or 10 minutes per 1lb/450gm. Crabmeat is also available frozen and tinned from supermarkets. It is very good for stir-frying.

GETTING OUT THE MEAT

A cooked crab that you dress yourself will probably be more succulent than one ready prepared, but it is important to check that the meat is fresh before you eat it.

• Twist off claws and legs.

• Lay crab on its back, tail towards you. Twist off tail flap, then prise off the piece of shell to which the legs were attached. The brown crab meat inside the body is exposed. If this is greenish or grey, or smelly, throw the whole thing away.

• If the meat is good, next discard stomach sac (behind the mouth) and long, soft greyish gills (dead men's fingers). These are not edible.

• Break or cut the body in half lengthways, then scrape out the body meat from all the cavities using a skewer. The red coral inside a female is a delicacy.

• Turn over the undershell and remove meat from leg cavities.

• Next, break open claws (with a rolling pin or mallet) and legs and extract the white meat.

• For dressed crab, scrub out the shell with warm soapy water, then oil it.

SPIDER CRAB

Found along the south and southwestern coasts, this crab was once known colloquially as Granfer Jenkins in Cornwall. It has long legs which curl round like a spider's and a reddish coloured carapace covered in little knobs.

Spider crabs are not common in Britain — most of them are exported to Europe where they are highly prized, but they are sold at Billingsgate, so your fishmonger might be able to get you some. They are in season May–October.

VELVET CRAB

These are much smaller than the common crab, but quite fierce

Above Common crab. *Food Features*

and surprisingly strong, so watch out for the pincers. The meat, according to one Hebridean cook, is as sweet as lobster and the little crabs can be simply broken up and made into soup.

LOBSTER, CRAWFISH, DUBLIN BAY PRAWNS AND CRAYFISH

LOBSTER

This is one of the most expensive seafoods in the world and, weight for weight, the fishing industry's single most valuable catch, though quantities landed are not large. Lobsters are potted especially in Wales, the West Country and along the eastern seaboard; Bridlington, Whitby, Scarborough and Newlyn are all landing ports.

The common European lobster lives on rocky bottoms of the sea and is caught in pots, traps or creels. It is a rather beautiful inky blue or blue-green when alive, and only turns bright red when cooked. Lobsters can grow very large indeed — at one time specimens of over 40in (1m) were not unknown. These days, 12in (30cm) lobsters are more common. The season for lobster is April–November.

You will find lobster sold fresh in fishmongers and supermarkets. Sometimes lobster tails are sold separately (they are not strictly tails, but the abdomen sections). You may also see lobsters sold live (see p15, DISPATCHING LIVE SHELLFISH HUMANELY). Fresh lobsters should have undamaged shells and should feel heavy for their size. Lobster meat is also available frozen and in cans.

There is little point in buying this delicious, expensive seafood, only to drown it in over-flavoured sauces. The key note should be simplicity. Lobster can be grilled or baked, or

Below: Lobster salad, served in the shell. *Seafish Industry Authority*

the meat used for stir-frying. Lobster salad is a good way of enjoying the full flavour of the meat. Jane Grigson recommends a Welsh combination — lobster and laverbread.

EXTRACTING THE MEAT

This is easiest done when the lobster is still warm from cooking.

• First, snap off legs as close to the body as possible.

• Break legs apart and extract the meat, using a skewer.

• Twist off claws and break open with a mallet or rolling pin. Extract the meat.

• Lay the lobster on its back.

• With a sharp, heavy knife cut firmly down each side along the length of the lobster. Pull away and remove the bony underplate. Prise up the tail meat. Scoop out the brown meat from the body and head. Remove the grey feathery gills, the gravel sac behind the eyes and the black thread-like intestinal tract running along the tail. The soft grey-green liver (tomalley) can be saved, and any pink roe (coral) found in a female.

Below: Lobster, *crayfish and (lower right) native crayfish. Food Features*

Above: Cooked lobster. *Food Features*

CRAWFISH

The crawfish, or spiny or rock lobster, is not from the same family as the European lobster. The most obvious difference is that the crawfish lacks the lobster's massive front claws. It is a reddish-brown in colour and is caught along the coast of southern and western England. It is in season April–October. Prepare and cook it like lobster.

DUBLIN BAY PRAWNS

Despite the name, these are not prawns but a kind of little lobster (nor are they confined to Dublin Bay although at one time fishing boats landed large catches there). They are also sometimes called Norway lobsters or langoustines, while the fishing industry calls them nephrops (their Latin name), but once they have been shelled they are best known as scampi.

There was a time when British fisherman threw Dublin Bay prawns back in the sea because there was no demand for them, but they started to gain popularity in the 1950s and are now one of our best known seafoods. Where would the British pub lunch menu be without its scampi and chips?

Dublin Bay prawns are an important catch for Scottish fishermen who trawl for them or catch them in special pots. Millions of pounds worth are landed at Fraserburgh, Ullapool and Ayr each year.

Dublin Bay prawns are in season April–November. They can be baked, poached, steamed fried, grilled, or microwaved — all the things you do to a prawn, you can do to a Dublin Bay prawn. They are widely available frozen and ready-breaded.

CRAYFISH

These little freshwater lobsters used to be very common in streams and rivers. It is said the monks of medieval England were fond of them and introduced them to many rivers. Mrs Beeton suggests potting them. They make good soup, too.

The crayfish used for stocking lakes and still waters are a species originally from Turkey: the Serpentine in Hyde Park, London, has a flourishing population which is regularly fished and marketed at Billingsgate. The native crayfish, or signal, is an astonishingly fierce little creature with bigger claws.

PRAWNS AND SHRIMPS

PRAWNS

The common North Atlantic prawn is found in shallow coastal waters all around Britain, but commercial fisheries for the species are small and mainly off north and west Scotland. This little crustacean is almost colourless when alive, but changes to orangy-pink when cooked.

Most prawns are sold cooked and frozen, either peeled or whole, but buy them fresh and you will be surprised at how much more flavoursome they are. If you do buy frozen, check whether the weight includes the protective ice glaze. You can also get prawns canned and bottled.

Raw prawns can be boiled for about 5 minutes in plenty of salted water. Do not overcook them. After boiling they can be peeled and fried. Prawns make excellent seafood soups, and they can also be microwaved, baked in the oven or grilled.

To peel whole cooked prawns, simply pull away the head and unpeel the body shell, making sure you remove the dark filament which runs down the tail.

Sadly, many people's only experience of prawns is the dreaded high-street-restaurant prawn cocktail — watery meagre shellfish drowning in a glutinous pink bath. There are many better ways of enjoying prawns, and even prawn cocktail is good if properly made — use good quality mayonnaise thinned with a little single cream and a squeeze of lemon — nothing else.

Prawn and shrimp butters are traditional British savouries: the cooked shellfish are pounded to a paste (or whizzed in a blender) with butter and seasonings such as mace and pepper.

SHRIMPS

How many children over the years,

have spent happy hours dipping for shrimps in rocky pools by the seaside?

These, our smallest crustaceans, are found all round the coastline but are mainly fished in the shallow coastal waters of the Wash, the Solway Firth and around Morecambe Bay. All shrimps are sold ready-cooked these days.

The small brown shrimp is the one which comes from around Morecambe Bay and is used in the famous English shrimp paste and potted shrimps, and for traditional North Country shrimp teas. It is very fiddly to shell; the other common shrimp, which is pink, is larger. The brown shrimp prefers sandy bottomed waters, the pink shrimp rocky bottoms, but they are sometimes fished together. Fresh shrimps are mainly available February–October.

There is another species, the deepwater shrimp, which is larger still. It is sometimes called the deepwater prawn and is caught mainly in the northern North Sea. Many prawns sold in Britain are in fact this species.

Prawns and shrimps can be prepared in much the same way, though the smaller they are, the less cooking or heating through they need.

ESTABLISHED 1799.

JAMES BAXTER,
Fisherman & Smack Owner,
Morecambe
WHOLESALE & RETAIL

Shrimps caught by our own boats daily.

Picked & Potted Shrimps, also Lobster & Shrimp Paste

PINK AND BROWN SHRIMP
PICKED PRAWNS—A SPECI

*EXTRACT OF OLD ADVERTISEMENT FR
© CASTLES DIRECTORIES LTD. 1912*

Baxter's of Morecambe Bay have been making potted shrimps to a family recipe for nearly 200 years.
James Baxter & Son

By appointment to Her Majesty The Queen
By appointment to H.M. Queen Elizabeth The Queen Mother
Purveyors of Potted Shrimps

• Potted Shrimps •
Ingredients - Shrimps Butter & Spices
200 gms

THORNTON RD • MORECAMBE LA4 5PB • TELEPHONE 0524
JAMES BAXTER & SON

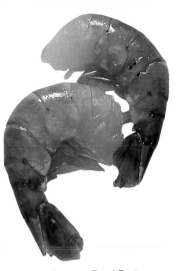

Above: Prawns. *Food Features*

SHRIMP PASTE

8oz/225gm shrimps (brown or pink)
8oz/225gm uncooked white fish
½ tsp/2.5gm powdered mace
½ tsp/2.5gm cayenne pepper
¼ tsp anchovy sauce
5oz/150gm butter

• Shell shrimps. Put shells and heads in enough salted water to cover and bring to boil, then strain out debris and use water to cook fish.
• When cool, put fish and seasoning in blender and whizz to a fine paste. Remove and mix with butter.
• Place mixture in saucepan, add shrimps and heat through.
• Place in pots and seal with melted clarified butter.

MOLLUSCS

OYSTERS, CLAMS AND COCKLES

OYSTERS

The oyster has not always been an expensive delicacy. In medieval times, and in the 19th century too, oysters were a cheap food of the urban poor: '...poverty and oysters always seem to go together....Blessed if I don't think than ven a man's wery poor, he rushes out of his lodgings, and eats oysters in reg'lar desperation' says Sam Weller in *The Pickwick Papers.* Traditional London steak and kidney pie and Lancashire hotpot always included half a dozen oysters.

In the late 19th century, overfishing created a scarcity, and oysters became prohibitively expensive. Happily, oyster farming and ranching (managing wild beds) have now brought down the price.

The common European oyster lives in shallow offshore waters and spends its life changing sex, depending on the temperature and feeding conditions. It is found all round the coast, but is commercially cultured especially in the Southeast and Cornwall.

The other kind of oyster commonly available is an introduced species, the big Pacific oyster, or giga.

If you see 'native oysters' for sale, you know they have been reared from British stock, as have Royal Whitstable oysters. Whitstable oysters

Above: Scallop. *Food Features*

will probably have been raised from French stock. Colchesters and Pyefleets are both from the River Colne in Essex. Oysters are sized, like eggs, from 5 (small) to 1 (large).

Ostreophiles recommend eating oysters raw, served on a bed of ice with citrus juice and a sprinkle of cayenne or Tabasco, but they can also be baked, fried in butter, added to soups and sauces, poached, grilled or barbecued in their shells.

European oysters are available September–April (when there is an 'r' in the

Citrus oysters. Classically eaten raw, oysters are also excellent cooked. Here they have been poached in orange juice, then combined with bread-crumbs, orange rind and scrambled eggs and topped with breadcrumbs, then flashed under the grill to crisp. *Seafish Industry Authority*

Left: Clams.
Food Features

Above: Oyster farm on a Scottish sea loch.
Association of Scottish Shellfish Growers.

Above: Oysters. *Food Features*

Above: Cockles. *Food Features*

month), gigas all year round. If you have never opened an oyster, get your fishmonger to show you as it is quite tricky. If you have no oyster knife, a screwdriver will do. Oysters keep well in the freezer for up to three months, and have the added bonus that when defrosted will automatically open.

Are oysters an aphrodisiac? There is no proof either way, but some people say it is the sensuous slurping of the flesh and the juices from the shell which give them their reputation, others that it is the valuable mineral trace elements they contain such as zinc.

CLAMS

Like oysters, clams are bivalves — they have two shells hinged together which they open and shut to filter food from the water. They do not move about much, but live in shallow intertidal waters where they are hand picked or dredged, mainly in the Solent.

The various different species of clam range from ½–4in(1–10cm); some have smooth shells, some ridged. The best known are carpet shells and various species of venus shells. Clams are available all year, but you may have to ask your fishmonger to get them for you. They are usually steamed gently until they open. Or they can be baked, braised, fried, poached or microwaved. Small clams are sometimes eaten raw.

COCKLES

These little bivalves are found all round the British coast, especially in estuaries. They were tremendously popular in the 19th century, particularly in Wales and Ireland where they were cried in the streets 'alive, alive o'.

South Wales is still a centre for cockling, especially around the Gower peninsula where it is carried out by hand — digging, raking and sieving, though Land-Rovers have now replaced the horses and carts which up until 20 years ago carried the haul back off the sands to the boiling sheds.

Leigh-on-Sea at the mouth of the River Thames is another source of cockles, and East Anglia is also famous for them — especially the large blue-grey shelled Stookey Blues from Stiffkey. The big Stookey shells were at one time cleaned and used to cook little sponge cockle cakes. Eventually someone decided to make metal tins in the same shape, and you can still sometimes see shell-shaped metal bun tins. Welsh cockle cakes, *teisen gocos*, are a different thing altogether — deep-fried cockles in batter, eaten with buttermilk.

Cockles are usually sold cooked. They are in season May–December. They can be used in soups or pies, as a traditional stuffing for Welsh roast lamb, tossed in with a pan of crisply fried bacon or mixed with other seafoods. They can also be baked, braised, stewed or microwaved. And you can buy them canned and bottled.

COCKLE PIE (pastai gocos)

4 rashers streaky bacon
1 onion, chopped
1½ pints/850ml cockles, soaked overnight and drained
¾ pint/450ml basic white sauce (made from 1oz/25gm butter, 2 tbsp/40ml plain flour,
1 pint/575ml milk, salt, freshly ground black pepper, freshly grated nutmeg)
8oz/225gm shortcrust pastry (made from 4oz/110gm plain flour, 4oz/110gm, margarine,
2-3tbsp/40-45ml cold water)

• Fry bacon till cooked but not brown, then dice
• Sauté onion in a little butter, till soft but not brown
• Boil cockles in clean water till they open
• Place bacon, onion and shelled cockles in a pie dish, season, then pour in white sauce
• Cover with shortcrust pastry and bake 375°F/190°C/mark 5 till golden-brown; about 40min.

Scottish rope-grown mussels. The mussels attach themselves securely to the ropes by threads secreted from a special gland — these threads are the 'beard', which is removed before cooking.
Association of Scottish Shellfish Growers

MUSSELS AND SCALLOPS

MUSSELS

These beautiful blue-black shellfish, with bright orange flesh, are found all around our coast, but almost all mussels that reach the market are farmed commercially in North Wales and the Wash in East Anglia, and from Scottish lochs where they are grown on ropes hanging from floating rafts. The mussel attaches itself securely to the rope by threads secreted from a special gland — these threads are the beard which is removed before cooking. Rope-grown mussels are particulary meaty and succulent, with no grit.

If you are planning to gather your own mussels, or any other shellfish, it is important to choose the right place and time, and to avoid polluted waters. Follow the simple rules for gathering and checking shellfish (pages 15). The red tides which affect mussels in the northwest during the summer are well publicised.

The best insurance against stomach upsets is to buy your mussels from a reputable fishmonger. They will probably be plumper and more succulent than those you gather yourself anyway. Wild mussels are available September–March; farmed mussels all year. Mussels should be bought tightly closed, or close when tapped. Discard open specimens before cooking and any which seem too heavy — they are probably full of mud.

Scrub the mussels, remove the beard, check them, discarding open specimens (see page 14) then put in a pot with a little liquid and steam till they open. Discard any closed specimens. The liquor, once strained, can be used for stock. Alternatively, they can be prised open before cooking.

A traditional Scottish way with mussels is to pull the crumb from hot rolls, butter, then pack the cooked mussels into the cavities. Wrapped in a clean handkerchief, these rolls made the perfect portable lunch for men going out to the fields or factories.

Mussels go well in soups, chowders, casseroles and pies, with rice or scattered over pasta. They can be baked, braised, poached, stir-fried or microwaved. Do not overcook them, or they will be tough. Mussels are also available cooked and frozen, and in jars and cans.

Above: Mussels.
Fish supplied by Tesco. Food Features

and again by opening and closing their valves. Most scallops come from Scottish waters, although they are also dredged from the English Channel and around the Isle of Man. Some scallops are farmed, and the industry is expected to grow.

SCALLOPS

There are two main kinds of scallops — kings and the smaller queens. Queen scallops, or queenies, are a completely different species from kings and have two curved shells, unlike kings which have one flat and one convex. Young queen scallops are known as princesses and are smaller still.

Unlike mussels, which live stationary lives firmly attached to rocks or seaweed, scallops live on the seabed and shoot about every now

PREPARING SCALLOPS

Scallops can be put convex side down in a hot oven for a few moments to open them, or prised open with a stout knife. Once open, pull the shells apart. Slide the knife around the grey outer frill of flesh — the skirt. This can be used for stock. Inside the skirt are the best parts, the white muscle and the pink coral. Separate these. The black intestinal thread is discarded.

Scallops are good baked, grilled, poached, steamed, stir-fried, sautéed or microwaved, or used in mixed

Scottish farmed scallops grown in a lantern basket. *Association of Scottish Shellfish Growers*

WINKLES AND WHELKS

WINKLES

The winkle, or periwinkle to give it its full name, is our smallest shellfish. Its tiny grey, brown or green conical shell yields the minutest mouthful of meat, which is extracted with the help of a long pin.

Winkles are found in rockpools along the shoreline and are still gathered by hand from designated areas. It is a backbreaking and often chilly job. Scotland is our main source of supply — more than 300 tonnes, over £150,000 worth, were harvested from the Ayr district in 1990. Rather confusingly, winkles are sometimes called whelks in Scotland, while whelks are known as buckies.

These days winkles are always sold ready-boiled, but if you ever gather your own (see page 15 on gathering shellfish), boil them for 5–10 minutes.

Winkles have always been plentiful, cheap and a favourite among Londoners who bought them freshly cooked from whelk and winkle stalls and ate them sprinkled with vinegar while promenading along the seafront at Clacton or Southend. Prim Victorian cookery authors considered them irredeemably vulgar and refused to talk about them.

Winkles can be fried, or microwaved, used in mixed seafood dishes, stirred into a pan of crisply fried bacon, Welsh-style, or added to

seafood dishes. The pretty ridged shells make good baking or serving dishes. A Manx recipe for queen scallops suggests filling the shells with cooked scallop pieces and a cheese sauce made from the milk in which the scallop pieces were simmered, all topped with breadcrumbs and cheese then browned under the grill; another recipe suggests raspberry sauce for 'Blairgowrie princesses'. Wild scallops are mainly in season September–March; farmed scallops all year. Do not overcook these delicate shellfish.

a sauce or soup. Best of all, steam them for a few moments to heat them through, then put a dish of them in the middle of the table, provide a loaf of crusty bread, butter, vinegar and some long pins, and just eat. You can buy winkles bottled in brine and canned, but they are available fresh September–April.

WHELKS

Larger than winkles, whelks are caught from the sea in baited pots or baskets; some Kent fishermen use converted milk crates to catch them. Wells-next-the-Sea in Norfolk probably has the most famous whelk fishery in Britain, but they are also landed in Scotland and the West Country.

Like winkles, whelks are usually sold ready-cooked. Raw whelks should be boiled for 10–15 minutes — it is important not to overcook them. The flesh is removed using a thin skewer or large pin. Whelks were at one time sold at whelk stalls and in pubs all over London and by the seaside. Sadly, crisps and peanuts have largely supplanted them as handy pub snacks. Whelks are in season February–August.

RAZORS, LIMPETS AND ORMERS

RAZOR-SHELLS

These are in fact a kind of clam with long shells which look like old-fashioned cut-throat razors. You often see empty broken razor-shells washed up on beaches.

Razor-shells are still something of a local delicacy in Wales, and in the Hebrides and the Orkneys where they are known as spoots. They are found live on clean sandy beaches, and traditionally are caught by pouring salt down the breathing hole left when the razorfish buries itself in the sand at low tide. The shellfish then comes straight out and must be grabbed before it disappears again. By all accounts, this is easier said than done.

Razor-shells need to be washed thoroughly to remove the sand, then steamed for a few moments to open them. Discard the shells, cut off each end, and the remaining 1½in/6cm of meat can be used in any recipe calling for clams. A typically Scottish method is to roll them in oatmeal and then fry in butter. In Wales they are baked in their shells and dressed with lemon and butter. Alternatively, they can be poached, steamed, used in soups, braised, baked or microwaved. Be sure not to overcook them or they will become rubbery.

LIMPETS

These are a traditional shellfish which never appear in shops. They are gathered by sharply knocking them from their toeholds on rocks, a technique that requires swiftness, accuracy and a bit of practice.

Limpets were once quite popular in Cornwall, where they were known as crogan, and in Scotland where they were often fried or boiled. As with all shellfish, if you are gathering your own make sure you are doing so in a safe, unpolluted area (see p 15).

ORMERS

Also called earshells, these molluscs were once everyday food of the people of Guernsey and Jersey. They are now quite rare, and a highly prized gourmet food. There has been an attempt to start farming ormers in recent years.

About 4-5in/10-12cm long, with rough, grey elongated shells, these shellfish are gathered from rocks at low tide. They are removed from their shells, the entrails discarded, then the meat is soaked and scrubbed till white and firm, then beaten to tenderise it. The ormers are then dusted with flour and fried or, after quick frying, casseroled with bacon or belly of pork, parsley and seasoning.

SQUID AND OCTOPUS

SQUID

These torpedo-shaped creatures are sometimes called calamari, inkfish or torpedo fish. They really are shellfish, but have a much-reduced shell which is found inside their bodies. This is known as the pen and is a transparent tube which has to be removed.

Squid are caught all around Britain, normally by trawl or seine net and often as incidental catches with white fish. Various species are fished and marketed at different times of year in different areas, but the most common is the northern squid which grows to 14–24in (35-60cm). Landings are not always predictable, as squid are a short-lived species and each year's catch is dependent on a particular breeding season — so buy them when you see them.

Much of our squid is exported, but it has become more common in fishmongers in recent years, and it is also found cooked on delicatessan counters. Fresh squid are often sold ungutted. To prepare them, first rinse under cold running water. Next, pull the head and attached innards out of the body sac. Cut off the tentacles and reserve; throw away head and innards. Pull the transparent pen out of the body sac, then remove the mottled skin. Reserve and skin the triangular fins, which are edible. Remove mouth part (beak) from centre of tentacles.

Most cookery books recommend that the body sac is cut into rings to be cooked. I find that children and squeamish adults look more

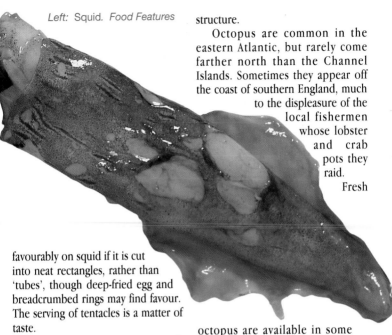

structure.

Octopus are common in the eastern Atlantic, but rarely come farther north than the Channel Islands. Sometimes they appear off the coast of southern England, much to the displeasure of the local fishermen whose lobster and crab pots they raid.

Fresh

favourably on squid if it is cut into neat rectangles, rather than 'tubes', though deep-fried egg and breadcrumbed rings may find favour. The serving of tentacles is a matter of taste.

It is important not to overcook squid — stir-frying is a good method, and only cook it till it turns from translucent to white, a few minutes, no more. The body sac is perfect for stuffing — use a robust stuffing mixture, one with capers and anchovies, perhaps, then braise in sautéed onions and wine or tomatoes. Squid can also be deep-fried or microwaved. Frozen, prepared squid are usually available, and you may find ready battered 'calamari' rings.

OCTOPUS

The octopus is a shellfish that has lost its shell altogether, and does not even have the squid's internal 'pen'

octopus are available in some fishmongers; they are in season May–December. You can tell octopus from British waters, because it has a single row of suckers on each tentacle. This species has to be beaten with a mallet to tenderise the flesh, then cooked slowly for several hours. Poaching or casseroling are good methods. More compliant species can be cooked like squid.

To prepare octopus, first cut away the tentacle section, then turn the head inside-out to remove the innards. Next, remove the beak. The octopus then has to be parboiled before the skin can be stripped away.

SMOKED FISH

HADDOCK AND COD

Haddock does not salt down as well as cod, so smoking has always been the main of way of preserving it. In Scotland, home of the wee haddie, curing and cooking it is a tradition and craft.

Above: Finnan Haddock and Arbroath Smokies. Fish supplied by Tesco. Food Features

FINNAN HADDOCK

This is the best-known cure of all, the famous Finnan (Findon) haddock which gets its name from Findon, a village just south of Aberdeen, although originally, it was neighbouring Inverbervie which was the haddock-smoking centre, and the fish were then called Bervie haddies.

In the early days, the haddock were heavily smoked with peat and sphagnum moss from the

KEDGEREE

This is an 18th-century dish which came from India at the time of the East India Company. It became popular in Victorian times as an addition to the breakfast sideboard — in those days breakfasts were substantial affairs, not to be taken lightly. We don't bother much with breakfast these days, but kedgeree makes an excellent Sunday brunch or light supper dish.
Seafish Industry Authority

serves 4
1lb/450gm smoked haddock, fresh or defrosted, skinned and flaked
6oz/175gm long-grain rice (basmati is best)
1–2oz/25–50gm butter or margarine
1 tbsp/20ml medium curry powder
2 size 2 eggs, hardboiled and shelled
2oz/50gm ham, diced
2 tbsp/40ml chopped fresh parsley
2 tsp/10ml lemon juice
salt and freshly ground black pepper
watercress, to garnish

• Cook the rice in ¾pt/450ml boiling water in a tightly lidded saucepan, for 10–12 min; 8min for basmati (bring to boil, then simmer on low heat, do not take off lid till cooked). Keep hot.
• Chop egg white and yolk separately. Set aside.
• Meanwhile, melt butter/margarine in a large pan, then gently sauté fish with curry powder for 5min. Stir in cooked rice, egg white and ham. Stir in lemon juice, sprinkle parsley over, and season.
• Garnish with chopped egg yolk and watercress.

surrounding moors, and ended up hard, dry and strongly flavoured. Then, Findon become the main centre, and when peat supplies ran low, wood-fired smoke kilns were used which produced the delicate cure we know today.

True Finnan haddock are headed and split down the middle with the central bone left in. They are the palest lemon colour, with no added colouring. This is a cold-smoke cure — the process does not heat the fish sufficiently to cook it.

GLASGOW PALES AND EYEMOUTHS

Glasgow pales and Eyemouths are similar to Finnan haddock, but even more lightly smoked so are the palest straw colour.

Finnan haddock (or Eyemouths or Glasgow pales) are best served grilled or poached with a knob of butter and freshly ground black pepper. Finnan haddock is also the basis for cullen skink, an old Scottish fisherman's soup (skink simply means soup or stew). It is made from Finnan haddock, fish stock, finely chopped onion, milk, butter, pepper and enough mashed potato to thicken it. Some people add a dollop of cream for good measure. If you can, use real undyed Finnan haddock.

Below: Fish hanging up to dry inside a Shetland crofter's cottage. The picture was taken some time between the 1890s and 1910. *Shetland Museum, Lerwick*

Right: Fish, possibly haddock, laid out on the beach to dry at Wadill Ayre, Burravoe in Shetland. After gutting and salting, the fish were dried in the sun on a stony beach, then built into a stack called a steeple. This photograph was taken some time in the late 1890s. *Shetland Museum, Lerwick*

Clockwise: Finnan haddock; smoked cod with colour; smoked cod without colour; golden culets (haddock). All these have been cold-smoked, at below 33°C, to avoid cooking the flesh and are still essentially raw. *Seafish Industry Authority*

Arbroath smokies. These have been hot-smoked, at 70-80°C, so need no further cooking.
Seafish Industry Authority

ARBROATH SMOKIES

Arbroath smokies, or pinwiddies, are another old Scottish cure. Small haddock are headed and left whole, then smoked to a coppery gold. Smokies originated in the fishing village of Auchmithie, between Arbroath and Montrose; the fish were originally smoked in pits in the ground using oak and silver birch wood chips. Unlike Finnan haddock, they are hot-smoked, so need no further cooking and can be eaten cold with salads, or simply grilled with a knob of butter.

Until recently, many fish counters, especially in the south, only sold brightly dyed smoked haddock. Now the undyed product is increasingly available too. You can also buy

Above: Smoked haddock, dyed and undyed. *Fish supplied by Tesco. Food Features*

frozen smoked haddock, cutlets or fillets.

RIZZARED HADDOCK AND BLAWNFISH

Smoking was not the only traditional way to preserve haddock. Rizzared haddocks were simply hung out in the wind and sun to dry. Similarly, hazel haddocks, or yardarm fish, were hung up on the rigging of ships. A similar Orkney cure for whiting, codling, coley, or indeed haddock, is blawn (wind-blown) fish. The fish are cleaned and rubbed with salt, then hung out in the wind overnight. Spelding is another name for wind-dried whiting and haddock, traditionally cured in seawater.

COD, LING AND WHITING

These are also sometimes available cold-smoked and can be used in most recipes for smoked haddock. Look out for smoked cod, especially the undyed variety, which is sold in many fishmongers.

HERRINGS AND MACKEREL

RED HERRINGS

In medieval times, vast quantities of salted and smoked herring were eaten, especially red herrings which were heavily salted, dried and smoked.

Proper red herrings are hard to come by. They are still made by the Raglan Smoke House, Lowestoft, where they are salted for 72 hours and kept in the smokehouse for six weeks to effect a proper cure. A proper red herring must be soaked for a couple of hours in a mixture of milk and water to reduce the saltiness, before grilling.

BLOATERS

Historically, East Anglia has been a great centre for herring fishing and curing — in medieval times Great Yarmouth held an annual autumn herring fair where thousands of barrels of pickled herring changed hands ready for Lent.

It was in Yarmouth that another cure for herring was discovered in 1835. The story (which may be apocryphal) is that a Mr Bishop, fishcurer, noticed his workers had left a batch of fresh herrings unprepared when they went home. He threw some salt over them then, pressed for time, popped them in the smokehouse. Next morning he tried one for his breakfast and was delighted by the flavour — the Yarmouth bloater had been

Shippam of Chichester have been producing bloater paste since 1894, and are now the only firm still making it.
C. Shippam Ltd

d i s c o v e r e d . Bloaters have a round shiny appearance and because they are usually cured ungutted, an almost gamey taste. They are good eaten with scrambled egg, cold with salad or made into another Yarmouth speciality, bloater paste, for tea. At the Bloater Shop, Gorleston-on-Sea, bloaters are traditionally smoked in a 200-year-old smokehouse.

KIPPERS

These are our favourite form of smoked herring. They were invented, it is said, in Northumberland in the 19th century when John Woodger experimented with a medieval cure used for 'kippering' salmon. He split and gutted the herrings, soaked them in brine, then oak-smoked them. People immediately liked the flavour, milder than red herrings.

Modern kippers are less salty than the 19th-century version, and because modern tastes demand a light cure, many kippers are dyed to give a deep red-brown kipper colour to the fish. Look out for undyed kippers though; they are available. Kippers are also sold frozen, as packets of fillets or goujons and in cans. Some of the best kippers come

from the Isle of Man and Loch Fyne in Scotland, where the herrings are large and fat and ideal for kippering.

BUCKLING

These are herring which are headed and gutted, then hot-smoked whole. Originally, it was the small lean Baltic herring, a sub-species of the common herring, that was used.

MACKEREL

Like all oily fish, mackerel is highly perishable, so pickling and smoking have been important traditional ways

Hot-smoked mackerel fillets, and peppered mackerel fillets.
Seafish Industry Authority

Grill, fry or poach kippers, or use an old method, and jug them: place in a jug of just boiled water and leave for 7–8 minutes. Kippers are hot-smoked so need only heating through. *Seafish Industry Authority*

of preserving it. Today, smoked mackerel is widely sold, and you will also find smoked fillets with peppercorns or herbs.

Mackerel is hot-smoked so can be eaten cold without further cooking. It is good for salads and makes excellent smoked mackerel pâté.

SALMON, TROUT AND SHELLFISH

SALMON

Salmon smoking is not a new technique — archaeologists think fishermen may have been smoking salmon over smudge fires nearly 4,000 years ago by the River Bann in Ireland. Medieval fishcurers usually preserved salmon by pickling it in brine, salting or drying, and though some was smoked, early methods produced hard, dry fish, very different from succulent modern cures.

Long sides of glistening, translucent smoked salmon are today the ultimate delicacy — a food for feasts and celebrations. Some of the best smoked salmon is still made in Scotland. Curers have their own family and regional recipes — some dry-salt the fish first, others soak the sides of salmon in brines flavoured with juniper, herbs, rum or other alcohol. The fish are then very gently smoked over oak, other hardwoods or juniper wood. Shavings from old whisky barrels are sometimes used, and are said to impart their own special flavour.

Most smoked salmon comes from farmed fish, though some wild is available. A word of warning — there are producers who pass off cold-smoked imported rainbow trout as salmon, even going so far as to sell it on salmon skin. Always buy from a reputable supplier; the Scottish Salmon Smokers' Association runs its own quality assurance scheme, and members display a round, gold sticker on their produce.

Unlike herring and mackerel, salmon is usually cold-smoked so is still raw when cured. But that is how it is eaten — uncooked, in razor-thin slices and a beautiful deep coral colour. Eat it unadorned with thin slices of good brown bread and butter and a squeeze of lemon. It is expensive, but because it slices so thinly, and is so richly flavoured, a

Smoked delicacies (left to right): eels; cod's roe without colour; cod's roe with colour; prawns; oysters; scallops, and, mussels.
Seafish Industry Authority

Smoked salmon money bag. In this elegant recipe, slices of smoked salmon are stuffed with fennel, diced red and green pepper and soured cream, then gathered at the top and tied with chive stalks. *Scottish Salmon Smokers' Association*

little goes a long way. Chop it into cream or curd cheese with a little dill and leave in the fridge for a couple of hours and the flavour will permeate right through. Or make smoked salmon pâté with butter, lemon juice and pepper. Hot-smoked salmon is available from some specialist shops.

TROUT

This is now widely available — many smokehouses produce it and most fishmongers and supermarkets sell it as whole fish, in fillets or as ready-made pâté.

Most smoked trout you see in shops is rainbow trout, but you may get sea or river trout from specialist outlets or by mail order. Inverawe Smokehouses in Argyll also produce smoked trout 'caviar', which they call botargo and say is unique to them. It is orange, and has a salty taste and texture, similar to caviar.

Above: Kippers. *Seafish Industry authority*

Trout can be hot- or cold-smoked. It makes a good substitute for salmon in pâtés and other dishes.

SEAFOOD

Other smoked seafood to look out for include smoked mussels, oysters, prawns and scallops, smoked eel and sprats.

SEAWEEDS

LAVER

This reddish-purple seaweed is found all around the coast, but it is a speciality in Wales. It used to be eaten in Scotland, too, where it was called slouk, made into slouk jelly and eaten with oatcakes by fishing communities. The Scots do not bother with it now but the Welsh still enjoy it and import supplies from Scotland to supplement their own stocks. Green laver is sometimes called lettuce laver.

Laver gatherers pluck the seaweed strands from the rocks where it clings at low tides 'like wet, brown silk'. At one time there were big drying houses along the shore which washed and processed the harvest. The industry today is a tiny fraction of what it once was, but you can still find laver sold in Swansea and Cardiff market, ready boiled and looking like puréed spinach. The centre of the industry is

Laverbread is often combined with seafoods; (clockwise) sea bass and seaweed sauce, gratin of oysters with laver and Stilton, laverbread quiche, Welsh lamb with laverbread and orange sauce, poached salmon and beurre blanc with laverbread, a traditional Welsh breakfast — bacon, laverbread and cockles, toasted laverbread fingers with sautéed herring roes and other toppings, smoked salmon, scrambled egg and laverbread. This recipe for laverbread quiche is from Colin Pressdee of the Welsh Barrow:

8oz/225gm shortcrust pastry
8oz/225gm lightly cooked mixed fresh vegetables — leeks, carrots, celery...
1 tsp/5ml mixed herbs
1 tbsp/20ml chopped fresh parsley
4oz/110gm laverbread
3 eggs
4oz/110gm low-fat cream cheese
½ pint/300ml milk
2oz/50gm cooked ham, diced (optional)
2oz/50gm cheddar cheese, grated (optional)
salt and pepper

- Line 12in/30cm buttered flan dish with thinly rolled pastry.
- Heat oven: 350°F/180°C/gas 4. Place baking tray in to heat.
- Mix eggs, cream cheese and milk till smooth and creamy. Mix in vegetables and laverbread; season and add herbs, and ham if desired.
- Pour into flan case. Top with grated cheddar if desired.
- Bake 15–20min or till cooked and golden.

at Penclawdd. You can also buy laver canned by a firm called the Welsh Barrow.

If you are harvesting your own, make sure you follow the rules for gathering seafood (see page 15), and use a reputable field guide. Do not take laver growing amongst the sand, as this is hard to clean. Rinse it initially in a clean rockpool, then when you get home, soak it in water for 2–3 hours changing the water five or six times to get rid of the sand. Next, it is slow-cooked for 5–6 hours till tender. It can be boiled (traditionally, it should be stirred with a silver fork), or put it in a large, lidded casserole dish and layered with knobs of butter, a little salt and a sprinkling of vinegar or lemon juice, then cooked in a slow oven. The resulting purée is, rather puzzlingly, known as laverbread — bara lawr — in Wales.

Traditionally, laverbread is rolled in fine oatmeal and fried in bacon fat, then eaten for breakfast, along with some good fat rashers. Laver sauce, a traditional accompaniment to Welsh lamb, is made by mixing the seaweed purée with Seville orange juice, butter and lamb stock. If you can only get sweet oranges, use half lemon juice. Laver sauce is also used as an accompaniment to sewin (sea trout) and other Welsh seafoods, and then cream is added in place of meat stock.

Laverbread, like other edible seaweeds, is loaded with trace minerals and vitamins; it was certainly considered a health food in the 18th century, when those who could afford to constantly overate and worried about diets. In Bath, where the fashion-conscious went to take the waters, potted laver was cried in the streets.

SAMPHIRE AND SEAKALE

SAMPHIRE

In the play *King Lear*, one of the characters peers over a huge cliff and exclaims in horror 'Half-way down hangs one that gathers samphire — dreadful trade!' Elizabethan playgoers were familiar with this green, fleshy plant which they ate in salads or pickled with cold fish and meat, though why Shakespeare thought perilous cliff-hanging was required to gather it is puzzling — it grows on beaches, mudflats and in marshes.

Today, we are not so familiar with samphire — it almost never appears in shops, though you sometimes see it on restaurant menus. It is common in East Anglia, especially north Norfolk where you might find it sold in local markets in July and August. Billingsgate often has it, so ask your fishmonger if he can get some for you.

The name was originally spelled sampier, from the French name Saint Pierre, but other names for the plant include glasswort, saltwort and pickle plant. The best samphire, says David Mabey, must be washed by every tide, so that is where you should harvest it. Make sure you have a good field guide and observe the rules for gathering and checking seafoods (see page 15).

The plants are cut at the base, washed in fresh seawater, then taken home for thorough washing in clean water. Eat the small young crunchy leaves in salads the Elizabethan way, or boil till tender and eat as a vegetable with melted butter — the traditional accompaniment for marsh-fed lamb or mutton. Alternatively, make pickle with it. It is sometimes called 'poor man's asparagus'.

SEAKALE

Another edible shoreline plant, which became very popular in the 17th and 18th centuries. By the early 19th century, many of our shingle shores had been stripped of the plants, which were taken to grow in gardens. Today it is a rare wild plant, so do not pick it.

If you want to taste seakale, grow it from seed in sandy well-manured soil. Seeds are available from specialist sources such as the Henry Doubleday Research Association's *Organic Gardening Catalogue*. Do not confuse it with Swiss chard, which is sometimes called seakale beet.

The blanched shoots of seakale are eaten in early spring when other freshly grown garden vegetables are scarce. Eat them raw, or gently steamed with butter.

CARRAGHEEN, DULSE AND KELP

CARRAGHEEN

The delicate purple-blue fronds of this pretty seaweed can be seen waving, fan-like in the water, from the seashore rocks to which it anchors. When the tide goes out it is left, a reddish brown, clothing the rocks of the mid-tide line. It is gathered from the Atlantic beaches of Scotland, and Ireland where the village of Carragheen gave it its name, along with its other name, Irish moss. At one time it was widely used in Yorkshire too, and in the Southwest where it was known as Dorset moss.

Carragheen is our only edible seaweed used commercially on any scale. You can buy it dried in health food stores, or ready-cooked from ethnic fishmongers. It is also used by the food industry for clarifying wine and beer, making ice cream and desserts and as a vegetarian substitute for gelatine.

If you are gathering your own carragheen, summer is the best time. Take a good field guide and observe the rules for gathering seafoods (page 15).

Once gathered it must washed in 5–6 changes of water, then the tough central stems cut out. Next, it is spread out to dry in the open air until it bleaches from purple to pinkish white. Do not completely bleach it though, or you will lose the delicate oceany flavour.

Carragheen can be used as a vegetable or as an addition to soups and stews. Or it can be made into Carragheen Mould. This is a Hebridean version:

A generous handful of carragheen, washed, then soaked for 2 hrs to get rid of grit

1 pint/575ml milk

1–2 tbsp/20–40ml castor sugar (depending on the sweetness of your tooth)
1 large lemon, the finely grated rind (or used mixed lemon and orange rind)

• Put carragheen in a saucepan, cover with water and boil for 30min.
• Remove from heat, rub through a fine sieve to make a jelly-like liquid
• Boil milk, then add 3 tbsp/50ml of the jelly liquid. Mix in lemon rind and sugar to taste.
• Pour into a wetted mould and allow to set. Serve with whipped cream.
• Remove carefully from mould, top with whipped cream and decorate with sugar-dipped lemon slices.

In Ireland, the jelly liquor is sometimes added to fruits in flans or used for making seafood in aspic.

DULSE

The broad red leaves of this seaweed can be found growing on seashore rocks along the mid-tide line. Small amounts are still gathered in northern Scotland, especially on the islands, and in Ireland where it is called dillisk and was once chewed like chewing gum. Dulse is usually dried before packaging up for sale and is also available cooked from ethnic fishmongers.

This tough seaweed needs a lot of boiling before it is soft and edible. Cooked and stirred into mashed potato with butter, it is known as dulse champ in Ireland. It can also be shredded finely and added fresh to salads, or to soups and fish dishes,

and used to make jellies. *The Little Hebridean Potboiler*, a fascinating little cookbook from the Isle of Eigg, suggests *duileasg bree*, dulse soup. The fresh, washed dulse is boiled, then drained and seasoned with salt and pepper. Milk, lemon juice and butter are added, and mashed potatoes to thicken it. These are all simmered together, then served with more butter and lemon juice.

KELP

These are long brown ribbon seaweeds which can be seen fringing the sea at low tide. At one time the people of the Hebrides, who called them tangle, harvested and burnt them and exported the ashes as a source of iodine, nitrogen and potassium, and they are still gathered as a source of alginates. The sugary stems were once chewed by Hebridean children, as seashore sweeties, while the fine fronds were boiled as a vegetable.

The Japanese use kelp a lot — you may find it in health food stores or in specialist fishmongers. Use it in stocks or soups — it is full of nutrients. Added to beans, it is said to help them cook more quickly.

Kelp is harvested commercially in the Orkneys by a small firm called Oottashell. The pickers go out in boats and cut the seaweed from the water — sometimes divers are used, depending on the state of the tides. Back on dry land, it is sliced up thinly and pickled in vinegars with red tamari, before bottling. It is apparently good in sauces and on pizzas.

INFORMATION

USEFUL ADDRESSES

Association of Scottish Shellfish Growers, Polfearn, Taynuilt, Argyll PA35 1JQ (0186 62 454): information and recipes leaflets about Scottish shellfish (enclose sae), plus cookery demonstrations/talks on shellfish farming.

British Trout Association, 10 Barley Mow Passage, Chiswick, London W4 4PH: for recipe leaflets and general information about buying and cooking trout.

Fish Foundation, PO Box 24, Tiverton, Devon EX16 4QQ: for information and advice on nutritional benefits of eating fish; leaflet available (enclose sae).

National Rivers Authority, Rivers House, Waterside Drive, Aztec West, Almondsbury, Bristol (01454 624 400): for details of regional river authorities, river fishing licences and fishing seasons.

Scottish Salmon Board, Drummond House, Scott St, Perth PH1 5EJ (01738 635973): marketing arm of the Scottish Salmon Growers' Association for information on products and suppliers.

Scottish Salmon Bureau, PO Box 1033, Edinburgh EH1 2BJ (0131-229 8411): consumer helpline for general information on and recipes for farmed salmon.

Scottish Salmon Smokers' Association, 163C Cargo Terminal, Turnhouse Rd, Edinburgh EH12 OAL (0131 317 7329): information and recipe leaflets on Scottish smoked salmon.

Seafish Industry Authority, 18 Logie Mill, Logie Green Rd, Edinburgh EH7 4HG (0131-558 3331): for information about the British seafish industry, also consumer advice, recipe ideas and nutritional information, and leaflets on buying, preparing and cooking seafish and shellfish..

SHOPS, RESTAURANTS AND SUPPLIERS MENTIONED IN THE BOOK

Harry Ramsden's Fish and Chip Shop, White Cross, Guiseley, W Yorks LS20 8LZ (01943 874 641): traditional fish and chips. Branches in eight other cities, and still expanding.

Rothay Manor Hotel, Rothay Bridge, Ambleside, Cumbria LA22 OEH (01539 433605): potted char and poached char on the menu in season.

F. Cooke & Sons Eel and Pie Shop, 41 Kingsland High St, London E8 2JS (0171-254 2878): traditional eels, pies and mushy peas, jellied eels and fresh eels to take home to cook.

James Baxter & Son, Thornton Rd, Morecambe, Lancs LA4 5PB (01524 410 910): Morecambe Bay potted shrimps by mail order.

Raglan Smokehouse, Raglan St, Lowestoft, Suffolk NR32 2JP (01502 581929): fresh and smoked fish including traditional red herrings and bloaters.

The Bloater Shop, 66 Englands Lane, Gorleston-on-Sea, Norfolk (01493 602884): traditionally smoked bloaters and other seafood.

Inverawe Smokehouses, Taynuilt, Argyll, Scotland (0186 62 446): smoked salmon, trout, botargo, eel by mail order.

The Welsh Barrow, PO Box 218, Mumbles, Swansea SA3 4ZA: tinned laverbread by mail order.

The Organic Gardening Catalogue, Chase Organics, Coombelands House, Coombelands Lane, Addlestone, Surrey KT15 1HY (01932 820958).

Oottashell Seafoods, East House, Easter Park, Holm, Orkney KW17 2SD (0185 678 428): pickled kelp by mail order.

BIBLIOGRAPHY

All About Cookery, Beeton, I. (Ward, Lock & Co, 1915 edn)

The Book of Household Management, Beeton, I. (S. O. Beeton 1861)

British Cookery, Grigson, J. (Michael Joseph)

Buyers' Guide to Food and Drink from the Highlands and Islands (Highlands and Islands Enterprise, 1993)

Cassell's Country Cookbooks — The Cotswolds, Wright, C. (Cassell, 1975)

Cassell's Country Cookbooks — The West Country, Wright, C. (Cassell, 1975)

Cassell's Shilling Cookery, ed Payne, A. G. (Cassell, 1894)

The Compleat Angler, Walton, I., ed Bevan, J. (J. M. Dent, 1993)

A Cook's Tour of Britain, The WI and Smith, M. (Willow Books, 1984)

English Food, Grigson, J. (Macmillan, 1974)

Fish and Shellfish, (Time-Life, 1979)

The Fish Book, Perry, K. (Chatto & Windus, 1989)

Fish Cookery Made Easy (Marshall Cavendish, 1979)

Fishes of the Sea, Lythgoe, J. & G. (Blandford Press, 1971)

Fishing — the Coastal Tradition, Marshall, M. W. (Batsford, 1987)

Floyd on Britain & Ireland, Floyd, K. (BBC Books, 1988)

Food and Drink in Britain — from Stone Age to recent times, Wilson, C. A. (Penguin, 1984)

Food Focus 2 — A guide to sources of fresh, lightly processed and speciality foods in the UK, Hurst, B. (Food from Britain, 1989)

Food in England, Hartley D. (MacDonald and Jane's, 1979)

Food in History, Tannahill, R. (Paladin, 1975)

The Food of the Western World, Fitzgibbon, T. (Hutchinson, 1976)

A Fresh Taste of Britain (Grub Street, 1989)

Freshwater Fish of Britain, Ireland and Europe, Phillips, R. & Rix, M. (Pan, 1985)

Game Fishing, the Guinness Guide to, Currie, W. B. (Guinness Superlatives, 1980)

Good Things in England, White, F. (Jonathan Cape, 1932)

The Guide to Seafish (Seafish Industry Authority)

In Search of Food, Mabey, D. (MacDonald & Jane's, 1978)

Introducing Macrobiotic Cooking, Esko, W. (Japan Publications, 1978)

Key Indicators (Seafish Industry Authority, Winter 1993)

Larousse Gastronomique, Montagne, P. (Hamlyn, 1965)

The Little Hebridean Pot-boiler — a Seashore Cookbook (Cleadale Crafts, 1990)

Mediterranean Seafood, Davidson, A. (Allen Lane, 1981)

The National Trust Book of Fish Cookery, Williams, S. P. (National Trust, 1988 reprinted 1991)

North Atlantic Seafood, Davidson, A. (Penguin, 1980, reprinted 1986)

Old Yorkshire Recipes, Poulson, J. (Hendon Publishing, 1974, reprinted 1992)

The Roman Cookery of Apicius, translated Edwards, J. (Rider & Co, 1984)

Sea Fisheries Statistics (Ministry of Agriculture, Fisheries and Food, 1992)

The Seafish Cookbook, Hicks, S. (Hamlyn, 1988)

Sea Fishes of Britain and North-Western Europe, the Collins Guide to, Muus, B. J. & Dahlstrom, P. (Collins, 1974)

Seafish Statistics (Seafish Industry Authority, 1993)

Seafood — a Connoisseur's Guide and Cookbook, Davidson, A. (Mitchell Beazley, 1989)

A Taste of England in Food and Pictures, Fitzgibbon, T. (Pan, 1986)

The Taste of Britain, Millon, M. and K. (Webb and Bower, 1985)

Torry Advisory Notes (HMSO)

Traditional Scottish Cookery (Robert Hale, 1973, reprinted 1993)

ACKNOWLEDGEMENTS

Among the many individuals and organisations I would like to thank for their help in preparing this book are:

The traders and officers of Billingsgate Market; Dr Ray Rice of the Fish Foundation; the Seafish Industry Authority; the Association of Scottish Shellfish Growers; the staff of Buckinghamshire county libraries; the Fisheries Statistical Unit of the Ministry of Agriculture, Fisheries and Food; Tesco Foodstores Ltd; the fishmongers of Aylesbury and Wendover markets.

Pictures, tables and artwork in the book are reproduced by kind permission of the following individuals and organisations:

Seafish Industry Authority; The Fish Foundation; Scottish Salmon Board; Steve Moss; Town Docks Museum, Hull; Harry Ramsden's; Scottish Fisheries Museum, Fife; Royal Cornwall Museum; Welsh Food Promotions; Ely Museum; James Baxter & Son; C. Shippam Ltd; Scottish Salmon Smokers' Association; The Welsh Barrow.

INDEX